SECRETS OF MODERN
POKER

Contrary to popular opinion, poker is not a game of chance or luck, but a scientific game of skill. You can add immeasurably to your fun in playing poker if you know how to play correctly. After a few hours spent with this book by two acknowledged card masters, you will be putting into practice your new-found command of the principles of the game. The change in your style of play will be imperceptible to your friends, but you will soon find that you are losing less and winning more often.

Played under the tutelage of Messrs. Reese and Watkins, poker is a game that will develop your understanding of the significance of odds and probabilities, your habits of clear and logical reasoning, and your ability to make decisions. This is a book that will get you to put your thinking cap on, too: For example, the game is draw poker with deuces wild; you hold two deuces and draw three cards. The poorest hand you can make is three eights, say the authors. Impossible, you say? It's true. Figure it out!

Here is a book that is full of sound advice—sage counsel gleaned in years of play all over the world, backed up with simple statistics and illustrated with examples of how to play your way through difficult hands. Here is modern poker as it is played in all of its forms and variations, with the stratagems and ruses to be employed and hints for assessing your opponents. If you have ever played poker—or if you want to learn to play or to play better—you will enjoy discovering the *Secrets of Modern Poker*.

how to
WIN AT
POKER

Terence Reese
Anthony T. Watkins

Published by
Melvin Powers

WILSHIRE BOOK COMPANY
12015 Sherman Road
No. Hollywood, California 91605
Telephone: (213) 875-1711 / (818) 983-1105

OTHER BOOKS OF INTEREST

How to Tell Fortunes with Cards

Blueprint for Bidding
Bridge Play
Bridge Players' Dictionary
Bridge Squeezes Complete
Complete Bridge Course
Develop Your Bidding Judgment
Duplicate Bridge
How to Improve Your Bridge
Play Bridge with Reese
Third Book of Bridge (Duplicate)
Watson's Classic Book on the Play of the Hand

Printed by

HAL LEIGHTON PRINTING COMPANY
P.O. Box 3952
North Hollywood, California 91605
Telephone: (213) 983-1105

"Secrets of Modern Poker" © 1964 by Terence Reese
is a revised edition of "Poker—Game of Skill"
© 1962 by Terence Reese and Anthony Watkins
Library of Congress Catalog Card Number: 64 - 15106

Printed in the United States of America
ISBN 0-87980-070-4

CONTENTS

CHAPTER ONE

HOW THE GAME IS PLAYED

Poker is one of the easiest games to learn and play. It possesses none of the intricate technique of bridge, for example. Starting to learn bridge from scratch, it would be three months before you could take your place in even a moderate game, but you could join in a poker game after three hours of instruction! And, if you were prepared to do some homework with this book, you would be a better-than-average player after a few weeks.

The essence of the game is simple. There can be any number of players from two to eight, but the usual number is five, six or seven.

One ordinary pack of fifty-two cards is used in actual play, though for convenience two packs are generally used alternately. After each hand the player on the left of the dealer should collect the cards so that when it is his turn to shuffle and deal there will be no delay.

The first dealer is traditionally chosen by any one player's starting to deal the cards face up. He deals until a Jack appears, and the player who gets the Jack is the first dealer. He shuffles, offers the pack to the player on his right to cut, and then deals. The first hand or "pot" is played. The deal then passes to the left, and the next pot is played. And so on.

1. THE POKER HANDS

The general object of the game is to get the best hand. Poker hands consist of five cards and are ranked in the following (descending) order:

1. **Straight Flush:** a sequence of five cards of the same suit. An Ace can be used at the beginning or end, but not in the middle of a sequence. Thus, A 2 3 4 5 and A K Q J 10 are both straight flushes. The second hand is called a **Royal Flush.**

2. **Four of a Kind** or **Fours:** four cards of one denomination and an odd card. 8 8 8 8 3.

3. **Full House:** three cards of one denomination and two of another. Q Q Q 6 6.

4. **Flush:** any five cards of the same suit. ◇ Q J 8 7 2.

5. **Straight:** A sequence of five cards, but not all of the same suit. An Ace can be counted high or low, but not in the middle of a sequence. ◇ 7 ♣ 8 ◇ 9 ♠ 10 ♡ J is a straight, but Q K A 2 3 is not.

6. **Three of a Kind, Triplets** or **Threes:** three cards of one denomination and two odd cards. 5 5 5 K 4.

7. **Two Pairs:** two pairs and an odd card. Q Q 7 7 3.

8. **One Pair:** a pair and three odd cards. J J A K 2.

9. **Five odd cards.**

The rank of cards is A K Q J 10 9 and so on. Unlike bridge, there is no distinction between suits. Hands falling within the same category are distinguished as follows:

Four of a Kind, Triplets and **Pairs,** according to rank; when pairs are the same, according to the highest odd card, and so to the fifth card.

Two Pairs, according to the higher pair; if these are the same, according to the lower pair; when both pairs are the same, according to the odd card. (Two pairs are said to be "Queens up" or "Nines up" or whatever the rank of the higher pair may be.)

Full Houses, according to the triplets.

Straights and **Flushes,** according to the highest card (except when an Ace is low in a straight). Thus, a "King-high straight."

Five odd cards, according to the highest card; when those are the same, according to the second card, and so to the fifth card.

Because the four suits have no relative value, if two or more players hold exactly equal hands (quite rare), they divide the pot.

(This section gives the classic rating of poker hands. In the Glossary at the end of this book, we mention special classes of hands to which special value can be assigned by agreement.)

2. STRAIGHT DRAW POKER

This is the basic Draw Poker game. It is played as follows:

Before the deal there is the "ante," a compulsory stake to start off the pot. Each player contributes one of the smaller chips in use. The dealer then deals the cards one at a time until each player has five cards. Everyone picks up his hand and examines it, and the first interval of betting takes place.

The player on the left of the dealer is the first to act. He has two choices, "passing" or "opening." He may open the pot by making a bet of, say, ten chips and putting that number of chips into the pot. Or he may pass, in which case the next player on his left has the same choice. If all pass, there is a re-deal and the ante is played for again. The ante may be "sweetened" at this time by one more chip from each player.

If one player opens, the player on his left has three possible choices: He may "fold," i.e., throw in his hand; he may "call" (also termed "see"), i.e., he puts in the same number of chips as the opening bet; or "raise" by putting in more chips than the opening bet. The players who originally passed opening may now choose to stay or raise when their turn comes again. If they do, they are said to "back in."

If one player makes a bet which no one calls, he wins the pot and collects all the chips without having to show his hand. The hand is over. If one player makes a bet which is called by one or more players and not raised by anyone, then the first betting interval is concluded.

The "draw" now takes place for all those who have stayed. Each player in turn, beginning with the player on the left of the dealer, may discard some of his cards and ask for fresh ones from the top of the pack. A player may also "stand pat" if he wishes; that is, he keeps his original hand and draws no new cards.

Now the second and final betting interval takes place for the players who have stayed for the draw. The opener is the first to act, or, the next survivor on his left. Each player in turn may either "check" or bet. A player who checks puts up no chips but reserves the right to call or raise if anyone else bets.

If everyone checks, the betting is over and the "showdown" takes place. The players still in the game lay their hands face up on the table, and the best hand collects the pot.

If one player bets, then everyone still in has the choice of passing, calling or raising. The betting continues until:

(*a*) one player makes a bet which no one calls. In that case, he wins the pot without showing his hand. Or

(*b*) a bet is made which is called by one or more players and not raised. In this case, the showdown takes place, and the best hand wins. Or

(*c*) raises and re-raises have reached a previously specified and agreed-upon limit of chips.

After the pot is won, the deal passes to the dealer's left. A new ante starts off the next pot.

3. FIVE CARD STUD

This is the basic form of Stud Poker, although it is waning in popularity. The ante is usually smaller than for Draw, often only one chip from the dealer. Stud is sometimes played without an ante.

After the ante, one card is dealt face down and one card face up to each player. Each player looks at his own concealed or "hole" card. The holder of the highest exposed or "up" card makes the first bet. When there are equals, the player nearest to the dealer bets first. An interval of betting follows in the usual manner, each player in turn having the right to throw in his hand (usually called "fold" in Stud), call or raise. Players who fold signify by turning their up cards face down.

When the betting has been completed, a third card is dealt face up to each surviving player, and another betting interval takes place, the player with the highest exposed hand being the first to act. Checking is allowed in all betting intervals except the first.

A fourth card is dealt face up, followed by another betting interval. Then the fifth and final card is dealt face up, followed by the fourth and final betting interval. If the final bet is called, the hole cards of the surviving players are turned up, and the best hand wins. Of course, the pot may be won at any stage of the game if one player makes a bet which no one calls.

4. SEVEN CARD STUD

This is a popular and rather wilder form of Stud, which is also sometimes called *"Down the River."* Two cards are dealt face down, four cards face up, an interval of betting taking place after each up card. The highest hand showing, as in all Stud games, is first to act, and checking is allowed in all but the first betting interval. The seventh and last card is dealt face down, and is followed by the fifth and final betting interval. The pot can also, of course, be won in any interval by a bet which no one calls.

5. OTHER VARIATIONS

There are many variations of Draw Poker. The best known is **Jackpots,** in which a player can open only with a pair of Jacks or better. **Lowball,** in which the lowest hand wins instead of the highest, has become extremely popular in the last decade.

Draw Poker can also be played with jokers. **Deuces Wild** is a form in which the deuces are used to represent any card in the pack. A fairly recent innovation is a joker (usually the joker furnished with the deck of cards) with limited powers and known as the "Bug." The Bug can be used only as part of a straight or flush or as an Ace.

There are variations of both Five Card Stud and Seven Card Stud. Either can be played low, or with wild cards, or with the Bug. Various other gimmicks are possible, particularly at Seven Card Stud, which lends itself to an almost infinite number of variations.

Poker is usually played "dealer's choice," the dealer being allowed to name the game. In a conservative, large-limit game the choice will probably be restricted to the three basic games of Straight Draw, Five and Seven Card Stud, plus Jackpots and Lowball. Even Seven Card Stud is sometimes banned. Small-limit games tend to allow more variations, and occasionally one comes across games where the dealer's choice is virtually unlimited.

A word of warning here. It is sometimes supposed that a large number of different variations take most of the skill out of poker. This is the opposite of the truth. The average player by simple observation and experience learns in time to play a fairly sound game so far as the ordinary forms of poker are concerned. But with variations that are played only occasionally and at long intervals, experience is not available as a guide. The general standard of play in these games is therefore much lower, and the premium on skill much higher.

All the main variations of Draw Poker (and also Straight Draw Poker), as well as both kinds of Stud Poker, will be discussed in detail in later chapters.

6. THE CHIPS

It is almost standard practice to have white, red and blue chips, the red worth five whites, the blue worth twenty whites. In large-limit games oblong yellow chips worth a hundred whites each may be added.

In small-limit games each player will usually start with a stack representing one hundred small chips; in a large-limit game two hundred is usual.

What these chips represent in money is obviously for the players to decide. The small chip may be valued at a penny, nickel or dime. It may be worth $1.00 or $100. The object of the game is to win chips, and what they represent in money is an incidental that affects the settling up after the game, but not the game itself.

7. THE ANTE

The object of the ante, the small compulsory bet which starts off each pot, is to give the opener something to play for. Practice varies, but for Draw Poker the ante is generally 1 or 2 small chips from each player. Stud, with four or more intervals of betting, tends to produce far bigger pots than Draw with its two betting intervals. To compensate, the ante for Stud is usually smaller, perhaps only 1 chip from the dealer. Sometimes Stud is even played without any ante.

We suggest that the following is the best system. For Stud, 1 chip from the dealer. For Draw, 2 chips from everyone, plus 1 extra chip from the dealer.

8. LIMITS

Although poker can be played with no restrictions on the size of bets, in practice a limit is always imposed. The limit controls the maximum size of the opening bet as well as the maximum amount by which a previous bet may be raised. A player can always bet less than the limit, but he cannot bet more.

The following are the various kinds of limit that may be enforced:

1. A **Flat Limit** of a fixed number of chips. A 5-chip limit is about the smallest that is ever played. This is sometimes modified into "five and ten," five before the draw and ten after the draw for Draw Poker. For Stud it means five in the early rounds, increasing to ten in the last round or at any time after the first round when a player has a pair showing on the table.

2. **Pot Limit.** A player may open for the size of the pot—that is, the total amount of the antes—and may raise a previous bet so as to double the total number of chips in the pot at that moment.

Example. The total ante is 10 chips. "A" opens for the size of the pot, 10 chips. There are now 20 chips in the pot. "B," if he wants to bet the limit, can bet 20 chips (10 chips to call "A's" bet and a further raise of 10 chips). There are now 40 chips in the pot. "A" can therefore re-raise the maximum by betting a further 40 chips, making a total of 80 chips in the pot. And so on.

Pot Limit is a very steep limit and is nearly always played with the overriding limit of Table Stakes as described below.

2A. **Half-Pot Limit.** Suppose there are 60 chips in the pot: the maximum raise is an additional 30 chips. Though not often played, this makes a good medium-limit game.

3. **Table Stakes.** Each player starts with an equal, agreed number of chips, generally 200, known as the "takeout." The only limit is that no one may stake more than he possesses in chips at that particular moment. If he runs out of chips in the middle of a pot, he gets a "free ride," i.e. he can stay in the pot without putting up any more chips. If he has the best hand at the showdown, he collects the stakes only up to the moment he began his free ride. The balance, or "side money," goes to the next highest hand.

Example. There are 100 chips in the pot. The players still competing are "A" with 60 chips left in his stack, "B" with 20, and "C" with 300. The game is Draw Poker and the draw is over. "A," with three Aces, bets 60 chips. He cannot do more than "tap," i.e., bet all his chips. "B" (who has a full house) can only call with his remaining 20 chips. "C" has three Kings and calls with 60 chips. Of the $100+60+20+60=240$ chips in the pot, $100+20+20+20=160$ go to "B" with his full house. "A," being higher than "C," collects the side money of 80 chips.

Originally Table Stakes was known as "Freeze Out," and when a player had lost his takeout he had to retire from the game. But in the modern game a player is allowed to replace his original takeout as often as he wishes, though he can only do this in between hands, not in the middle of a pot.

As already said, Table Stakes is often played in conjunction with Pot Limit, and this is the standard large-limit American game.

9. LARGE OR SMALL LIMITS?

A large limit makes more interesting poker than a small limit, and offers greater scope for skill. Contrary to popular belief, it does not necessarily mean high stakes in money. Of course, a lot of chips will change hands. Whereas in a 5-chip-limit game it would be difficult to lose more than about 500 chips in one session, at Pot Limit or Table Stakes it is quite possible for a player with exceptional bad luck to lose his original takeout ten times over, a loss of 2,000 chips. But the value of the small chip may be anything the players wish. If valued at 1¢, the loss would be only $20.00.

Of course, poker can be played without any values having been assigned to the chips. Much of the strategy involved in bluffing is removed, however, if players have "nothing" at stake in the game. We are not suggesting that poker should always be played for money stakes (it can always be agreed that the loser of the most chips will take everyone to dinner, for example), but merely pointing out that—as in any game—much of the fun of playing goes out of a game in which nothing is at stake.

JACKPOTS

We deal with Jackpots first, and in some detail, because they are widely played and exhibit principles that are common to all forms of Draw Poker.

The rules are as for Straight Draw Poker as described in the previous chapter, with the additional rule that you must have a pair of Jacks or better to open. If the opener does not have to show his hand at the showdown, he must still show his "openers" to prove he did have the minimum requirements. He may split his openers by, for instance, discarding one of an opening pair in order to draw to a four-card straight or flush. In this case, the discard must be shown on request. (In some games the opener must announce if he is splitting openers.)

1. OPENING

It is worthwhile to begin by looking at the odds (in round numbers) against any one player's being dealt a particular hand. They are as follows:

One pair	14 to 10 against
Two pairs	20 to 1 "
Threes	45 to 1 "
Straight	250 to 1 "
Flush	500 to 1 "
Full House	700 to 1 "
Fours	4,200 to 1 "
Straight Flush	65,000 to 1 "

The exact odds are not particularly important at this point, and are scarcely worth memorizing, but they explain why in the average deal no one has better than a pair, and nearly half the players don't even have that.

If you have openers, the chances are you have the best hand, but several of your opponents are likely to have lower pairs. If you open for a small amount they will all stay and draw cards, and since they all have as good a chance as you of improving their hands, a likely outcome is that one of them will improve, and you will not. You should, therefore, open for the limit up to the size of the pot. This will keep out the small or "short" pairs, and give your opening pair a reasonable chance of winning the pot even if you don't improve in the draw.

There is an exception to this rule, and that is if you are first or second to act in a seven-handed game, or first to act in a six-handed game. The player in such a position is particularly vulnerable and is said to be "under the guns."

Consider the position of the first to act in a seven-handed game, who is, of course, on the immediate left of the dealer. He has six players over him who may raise him. He needs extra strength in order to open, and should not do so with less than a pair of Kings. Second to act in a seven-handed game, or first to act in six-handed, is similarly in an exposed position with five players sitting over him. He needs at least a pair of Queens to open. Remember that checking on the opening round does not prevent any of these players from backing in later if the situation warrants it, unless, of course, no one else has opened.

Some players make a habit of checking when under the guns with a strong hand, say three Aces or better, with the specific intention of raising later. This is known as "sandbagging." The advantages are that they may catch several players for a raise before the draw. Also, they avoid playing the pot from the worst position of all, the opener's, who has to bet first after the draw. The disadvantage is that there is always a possibility that no one will open and the good hand will be wasted. Sandbagging in a Jackpot is something which should be done only occasionally, and only in a seven-handed game, where the odds are that one of the other six will have openers.

Splitting Openers

It sometimes happens that the opener has a hand like this:

♣ J ◇ J 6 3 5

Besides containing a pair of Jacks, the hand is also a four flush. The problem is, should the opener draw one card to the flush or three to the Jacks?

If someone has raised before the draw, suggesting that he holds two pairs, the opener should split his pair of Jacks. He is hardly likely to win the pot unless he improves to three Jacks, and by drawing three cards, he has only 1 chance in 9 of getting this. Better to take the 1 chance in 5 of making a flush.

However, if there was no raise before the draw, and if you have only one or two competitors, then a split is not justified, particularly if your pair is better than Jacks.

On the following hand the openers should always be split:

♣ Q ◇ Q J 10 9

This hand has a 1 in 3 chance of improving to either a straight, a flush, or a straight flush, and these possibilities are too good to waste.

In most games the opener need not declare that he is splitting his openers, but he must be able to show his discards at the end to prove that he opened legitimately. Always make a habit, therefore, of laying down your discards carefully in front of you, whether or not you have split. If you don't—if you only do this when you have a split, and otherwise throw your discards casually into the general litter on the table—then you might as well openly announce that you have split. And this may deprive you of any chance of bluffing out a pair if you miss out with your straight or flush.

2. PLAYING AGAINST THE OPENER

Every time you stay you make a bet. Whether the bet is a good one or not depends on the answers to these questions:

How much does it cost to stay?
How much is there in the pot?
What are my chances of winning the hand?

This is the eternal triangle that determines the play at this stage in all forms of Draw Poker. To take a simple example, suppose there are twenty chips in the pot and that it would cost you ten chips to stay. You would be getting 2 to 1 for your money. To make it a good bet, you would want to have 1 chance in 3 of winning the hand.

There is no problem in knowing how much it costs to play, and none in assessing how much there is already in the pot. As to that, you may wonder why you should not look forward to what the pot will eventually be worth: other players may stay and there may be some raises before the finish. That is true, but if you are going to make this assumption you must also take into account that you may improve, pay out more money, and still not win. These things balance out, so that on the whole it is advisable to base your calculations on the money at present in view.

What are your chances of winning? This is the third question and the only one of the three that presents a problem. Fortunately it is not a difficult problem to solve. All it requires is a knowledge of a few odds, the "draw percentages" as they are called.

We can best examine the matter by studying the play on various holdings.

Play of One Pair

Let us begin by considering the odds against improving a pair by making the normal draw of three cards. They are as follows:

5 to 2 against any improvement
5 to 1   "   Two Pairs
8 to 1   "   Three of a Kind
97 to 1   "   Full House
359 to 1   "   Four of a Kind

This table is interesting, but it doesn't tell you what you really want to know, which is what your chances are of beating the opener. He probably has a better hand than yours at the moment and, like you, he has chances of improving in the draw.

The average hand for a Jackpot opener is a pair of Kings, but in estimating the chances of beating the opener it would not be sound judgment to ascribe to him precisely that hand. Taking all things into account, the chances of a player's beating the opener after the draw are as follows:

With a pair of Jacks or smaller pair	4 to 1 against
With a pair of Queens	3 to 1 "
With a pair of Kings	Slight odds against
With a pair of Aces	Slight odds on

In a large-limit game, where the opener can, and almost invariably will, open for the size of the pot, it follows that you must think twice about staying with anything less than a pair of Kings. This applies particularly when you are sitting near an early opener and there is therefore a chance of a raise from a later player. If you are one of the last to act, the risk of a raise will have disappeared and you are ideally situated for the final betting if you do improve. Stay with Queens, and even take a chance occasionally on lower pairs. As the table shows, against the opener alone you have almost as good a chance of winning the pot with a pair of deuces (before the draw) as with a pair of Jacks. But if several players have stayed in a large-limit game, this indicates good hands around the table, and the last thing you want to do is to get involved with a small pair, however apparently attractive the odds in chips.

In a game where the limit prevents a pot-sized opening bet, a pair of Queens will generally be worth playing in any position, and, in the ideal position on the immediate right of the opener, almost any pair is worth taking a chance on. Again, however, if several players have stayed, which is not uncommon in small-limit games, a small pair is a poor proposition in spite of the excellent odds in chips. Suppose that as dealer you hold a pair of nines.

The ante is 14 chips, someone opens for 5 chips (the limit) and two others stay. There are 29 chips in the pot, and it will cost you 5 to stay, giving you odds of 29 to 5. This just about represents your chances of success. You may just win if you improve to two pairs, and probably will if you get three nines. But with a pair of fours the odds turn against you. Even three fours, if you get them, will be beaten almost as often as not, with three opponents.

The real trouble about playing low pairs is that even when they do improve, it will so often be only to second best, and in poker that is the worst possible place to occupy.

If you play as we suggest you will rarely run into a raise before the draw when you are holding less than a pair of Kings or Queens. These holdings can just stand only one raise. The raiser is marked, on the average, with two pairs, around Jacks up. He is unlikely to improve, and if you improve at all you will probably beat him.

A second raise before the draw should indicate three of a kind, probably high triplets, in a large-limit game. Your pair is hopelessly outclassed.

Play of Two Pairs

Two pairs is the most difficult combination to play. It is a good hand before the draw, probably better than anyone else's, but the odds are 11 to 1 against filling to a full house. Unimproved, two pairs have only a poorish chance of winning the average pot, particularly if they aren't high pairs.

The awkward thing about two pairs is that, brittle a weapon though they be, you often have to raise on the strength of them. That is because two pairs will seldom win if you have more than two opponents. Therefore, if you are close to the opener you should raise—not so much to swell the pot as to "protect" your hand by keeping down the number of competitors.

Here again we must make a distinction between high-limit and low-limit games.

(1) In a high-limit, seven-handed game, two small pairs are not

worth a raise and in the early positions are even a doubtful stay. However, two pairs Queens up or better are worth a raise at any time. Normally any two pairs are worth a raise in a five-handed game. If you are re-raised that is not so good, but, as we said, two pairs are hot to handle!

(2) In a low-limit game, you can play two pairs more boldly. A re-raise is not such a serious matter, and if you suspect a bluff you can stay to the finish without too great expense. Two pairs represent, when all is said, an average winning hand. Raise with any two pairs when you are near the opener. Farther around the table, if two or three players have stayed, you need Queens up to raise. With lesser two pairs you may be in a quandary. Consider the following example:

The antes total 14 chips, the limit is 5 chips. Someone has opened for 5 chips and three players have stayed in addition to the opener. You are last to act and have nines up. Against three or four competitors your nines up are unlikely to collect the pot and are not good for an ordinary aggressive raise. A raise of 5 chips won't protect your hand, for it will be met by most, if not all, of those already in the pot. However, it is just worth staying, for you are getting a good percentage, 34 chips to 5, which is probably not far short of your chances of winning.

If you raise with two pairs and are re-raised, you should normally retire. If the pot has already been raised and you are not yet committed, anything much less than Aces up is a doubtful proposition. In a small-limit game, you can be perhaps slightly less cautious.

Play of Three of a Kind

We need not stay so long with this hand. Whatever the circumstances, triplets are worth at least one raise before the draw. You are entitled to assume you have the best hand so far, and furthermore it will be to your interest, especially if you have low triplets, to cut down the field. You do not want to allow players who have higher pairs or four-card straights or flushes to enter the pot cheaply.

The only problem at this stage is when you have three tens or better and are sitting near the opener with four or five players to follow. If you raise you will probably keep them all out and the final pot will be a small one. If you simply stay you may encourage others to stay and may eventually manage to build up a big pot.

If the pot has already been raised, suggesting two pairs or low triplets, you can re-raise, though in a large-limit game it is as well to have three tens at least.

Play of Bobtails and Four Flushes

The odds against filling a four-card flush are just over 4 to 1. The odds against completing a bobtailed (open-ended) straight, for example 4 5 6 7, are just under 5 to 1.

In a large-limit game these odds will normally be present only when three or four players have stayed. In a small-limit game two or three competitors may give you the required odds in chips. For instance, if the total ante is 14 chips and the limit 5 chips, and if one player has already stayed, you can stay with a four flush or bobtailed straight, as you will be getting odds of 24 chips to 5.

An important difference between playing these hands and drawing to a pair or even low triplets is that you can add together the contributions of everyone in the pot without the feeling that your prospects of winning are seriously diminished as each new player comes in. When you have no more than a pair you come to value it less and less as the pot grows. When you draw to a flush or straight you hope to win the hand if you improve, and you therefore regard all the other players as potential victims. You can also expect to win some extra chips after the draw. For that reason you can stay with rather less than the odds theoretically require.

When you have a choice between drawing to a pair or to a four-card straight or flush, drawing to the straight or flush will usually be the better proposition except when you have only one opponent or when you have a high pair which may win without improvement.

A four-card straight flush should always be played, for it has a 1 in 3 chance of improving either to a straight, a flush or a straight flush. It is in fact generally worth a raise before the draw because of its excellent possibilities. But a three-card straight flush is worthless. So also is an inside straight, such as 4 5 6 8, or a closed or one-sided straight, such as A K Q J. The odds against their improving are 11 to 1, which are almost never obtainable.

A well-known gambit for the very bold is to raise before and after the draw on all their one-card draws. They will certainly have a lot of fun, but they won't make money against sound opposition. The counter is simply to call them every time, for the majority of their final hands are bound to be busted straights or flushes. On the other hand, it is sound tactics occasionally to raise a crowded pot with one to a flush provided you are prepared to follow up with a bluff if you don't fill. This may or may not come off, but even if it doesn't you can count on all your one-card draws being called for the rest of the evening, however high you bet.

Play of Pat Hands

First raise before the draw can be taken to mean two pairs, second raise, three of a kind. A pat straight is therefore worth a third raise, if you are lucky enough to get the opportunity. For a fourth raise you need a pat flush, preferably a top flush. For a fifth raise before the draw you need a full house or four of a kind. These are normal standards for large-limit play, though in an enthusiastic small-limit game you may get raises on much lighter grounds.

Sitting next or near to the opener with a pat hand, an objection to raising is that you may frighten the others out. It may well be best simply to stay and lure a few more victims into the pot.

Someone may even raise, enabling you to re-raise. In large-limit poker a really big pot is usually obtained by sandbagging at the right moment. In small-limit poker, where players don't scare so easily, that stratagem has less value. It is usually wise to follow the straightforward policy of betting out whenever you think you have the best hand. Often the opener himself, perhaps holding threes, will prove your best customer by re-raising.

3. THE DRAW

The normal draw is, of course, three cards to a pair, two cards to three of a kind, and one card to two pairs. But quite often a player will draw differently, either because he thinks an irregular draw will increase his chances of winning the hand or because he wants to conceal the exact nature of his holding. The second reason is much more common than the first, for only in special circumstances will you actually increase your winning chance by making any other than the natural draw.

Irregular Draws to Improve Chances of Winning

The simplest play of this kind is to draw two cards to a low pair and an Ace "kicker" (odd card). This may very slightly increase your chances of winning, at least in the extreme case of the pair being deuces or similar low cards. You have a slightly better chance of making Aces up with a two-card draw than three deuces with a three-card draw, and the one hand is obviously almost as good as the other. Again, if the opener draws one card, suggesting two pairs, and your hand is 6 6 A 4 J, you may ever-so-slightly increase your chances of winning by keeping the kicker. However, it is very close, and if there is another competitor besides the opener it will be better to draw three cards. (Probably it would have been better still if you had decided not to stay in the first place, with only a pair of sixes and an odd Ace . . .)

It is also possible to think up some rather special cases when it might be a good idea to break up two pairs. For instance, you have A A 7 7 J, and the indications are that the opener started off with three of a kind. Now you have a better chance of making three Aces by drawing three cards than of making a full house or triplets by drawing one card to the two pairs. If there is ever a time to split two pairs, this is it. But, after all, the opener once in sixteen times will make a full house, and it would be a calamity then if you gave up your best chance of making "Aces full." Many players follow the simple course of never breaking up two pairs.

Splitting a pair to draw to a four flush or bobtailed straight is a different matter. Unless you think your pair is high, you should always draw to the straight or flush against two opponents and very often against one. Remember, if you hold a pair of Queens against a pair of Aces it is 7 to 2 against your ending up with the better hand. But the odds against making a flush are not much more, and if you succeed you can bet out with real confidence after the draw.

Deceptive Draws

The most common example, so common that it scarcely ranks as a deception, is to draw one card to three of a kind. The trouble about raising before the draw with triplets and then drawing two cards is that so often your end bet after the draw will not be called. Drawing only one card may well increase your chances of being called. On the other hand, by drawing one card instead of two, you do cut your chances of improving from 9 to 1 against to 11 to 1. (Actually, you slightly increase your chances of getting a full house but halve your chances of getting four of a kind.) This is a powerful consideration when the field appears to be strong. Against one opponent who seems to have a pair, it is sound tactics to mask threes by drawing one card about half the time.

A rather pointless deceptive draw, which is nevertheless sometimes done, is to stand pat with two pairs. The idea is that this will inhibit an opponent with a good hand from betting after the draw, and so you reach the showdown cheaply. Maybe you will, but you still won't win the pot. It is surely better to take the 11 to 1 chance of making a full house with a one-card draw.

There are also, of course, deceptive draws which are part of an outright bluff. For example, you may decide to double the pot on a low pair; if your opponent stays, your best hope is to draw two cards and double again!

4. AFTER THE DRAW

If you have opened, and therefore have to make the first bet after the draw, you have the choice of checking or betting. If you judge that you have the weaker hand, you will naturally check. Even when you have good reason to suppose you have the better hand, it will often be good tactics to check.

Checking

The following are examples of sound checks:

(a) You open with a pair of Jacks, draw three cards, and end up with two pairs, Jacks up. Your sole opponent also draws three cards. Now mathematically the chances are that you have the best hand. But if you bet, your opponent won't call unless he has improved, and if he has improved he will probably beat your indifferent two pairs. Your bet is therefore unlikely to gain you anything and may well lose you something. "Don't bet two pairs after the draw," is a sound old poker maxim, at least so far as anything less than Aces up is concerned.

(b) You open with a pair of Aces and are raised before the draw by an opponent who draws two cards. You draw three cards and improve to three Aces. Here obviously is an occasion to sandbag. Your opponent is marked with three of a kind and probably hasn't improved (it's 9 to 1 against). If you check, he will bet, and you can raise.

It is necessary to say that in some games it is considered unfriendly to check and then raise. In such a case you would have to play the straightforward game of raising right away with your three Aces.

(c) Against a one-card draw who didn't raise before the draw and must therefore be suspected of drawing to a straight or flush, it is best to check even if you have three of a kind. If you bet, he won't call if he hasn't filled, and if he has filled he will beat you. So your bet can't gain you anything, and might lose you something. Your three Aces in this hand are really no better than two Aces!

Raising

Once the betting starts, whenever you think you have the best hand, raise. Leaving aside for the moment the question of bluff, it is not too difficult to make an informed guess as to the other man's hand. Each bet, taken in conjunction with former events, points to a certain class of hand. Consider, for instance, two three-card draws betting against each other. First raise indicates at least two pairs Aces up, probably three of a kind; second raise indicates at least three Aces (in a large-limit game); third raise a good full house, and so on. In the unusual event of two pat hands, first raise after the draw would indicate a flush, second a top flush or full house.

In a small-limit game raises can be made on much lighter grounds. It is almost true to say that you should raise whenever the balance of probability is that you have the best hand. In a large-limit game, where the risk of a possible re-raise is always a very serious matter, you want a fair margin in your favor. If you haven't got this, play safe and simply call.

If you do decide to raise, always raise the limit up to the size of the pot, if possible. The only exception would be the very unusual situation where you think that a limit bet would not be called but some smaller bet might be. Even if the limit allows it, for instance in Table Stakes, there is no point in betting more than the size of the pot. All bets must have some relation to the amount already staked, even in unlimited poker.

Calling and Dropping

Whatever your hand—good, bad or indifferent—there may come a time when you think you are outclassed. When this happens you have the awkward decision: to call or to drop out. If you *know* you are beaten, there is no problem. Drop out instantly, and don't waste any more chips. If you are genuinely uncertain, again there is no problem. You must call.

But most of the time you will be *fairly certain* that you are beaten, that your opponent is not bluffing, and it is then that the problem arises. In a large-limit game you can often save yourself a lot of money by having the courage of your convictions and going quietly. Most bets are genuine bets, and the man who says, "I'll call," loses most of the time. It is, of course, very easy never to be bluffed, but it can be very expensive in the long run and is the mark of a poor poker player.

In a small-limit game the situation is quite different. If there has been some brisk competition, the cost of calling the final bet may well be only a tiny fraction of the total pot. The percentage usually favors a call unless your chances seem utterly hopeless. One successful call will recoup the losses on four or five unsuccessful ones.

CHAPTER THREE

"TO HELL WITH PERCENTAGES!"

One of the authors remembers, with some shame, an incident that took place many years ago in a game in La Paz, Bolivia. He made a pretentious and extravagant remark on the subject of percentages, whereupon another player, a test pilot from Douglas Aircraft, said: "To hell with percentages! I play by the seat of my pants." As he had at that moment a far bigger stack of chips than the author, that ended the dispute.

In fact there is no dispute if the matter is considered logically. Skill in poker is partly technical—based on percentages—and partly psychological, and the comparative importance of each depends simply on the limit.

In a small-limit game, if you play a consistently sound technical game you get percentages working for you and your chips will slowly but surely accumulate, just as the profits of a casino or a bookmaker accumulate, and for exactly the same reason. Bluff, deception, psychology, these have only marginal importance. Small-limit Draw Poker is basically a matter of percentages, and the winner is the man who handles them best.

In a large-limit game, good technique is not enough. It will help in the small pots; indeed, it is essential, or you will suffer a steady drain on your chips. That test pilot may have played by the seat of his pants, but if so, he carried an efficient computer down there somewhere. But in a pot-limit game it is the big pots that count, the swings of hundreds of chips, and to be on the right side of these you need judgment, a flair for outthinking opponents, and the ability to keep them guessing.

This chapter is therefore primarily for the large-limit player.

1. THE PERSONAL FACTOR

Study Your Opponents

If watched closely, a beginner, or a very bad poker player, will sometimes give away information in an obvious, physical way. When he bluffs, there will be a difference in manner or voice. When he has a poor hand, he will look bored. When he picks up a good hand, or improves in the draw, he will suddenly take an alert interest in what is going on. In a table stakes game he may even be observed assessing the amount of chips held by a key opponent. The average player manages to avoid these elementary mistakes, but sometimes in his anxiety to avoid them, he may overact his part. An unnaturally impressive calm or an over-elaborate carelessness often indicates a really good hand, while an overwhelming appearance of confidence may well hide a bluff.

Some inference can generally be drawn from a long pause. It indicates some problem, and the nature of the problem may be fairly obvious. Similarly a very quick play, denoting absolutely no doubt at all as to the action to take, may be a useful pointer.

Some players like to arrange the four cards of a straight in order, and if they fill it or complete it, will carefully put the fifth card in its right place at the beginning or end or in the middle of the sequence. To the careful observer, this can be a dead giveaway. Another common mistake is for a player to draw to a straight or flush and then show by his immediate loss of interest in the proceedings that he hasn't filled. Sometimes a player will even go to the extent of throwing in his hand out of turn. This in itself may be useful information, but more valuable still is the knowledge that when this player later makes another one-card draw and does not act in this manner, he has made his straight or flush.

There is, however, a limit to the information that can be obtained from direct observation of this sort. Most of your opponents will know enough to play at roughly the same speed and in the same manner, while appearing to take more or less the same degree of interest in every pot (and this should be your aim).

Generally, all you have to go on is knowledge of the usual tactics of people you play with. Study them closely. Notice carefully what significance can be given to their bets. Are they liberal or cautious ? How much reliance can be placed on their draws ? Some players nearly always make the natural draw. Others go to the opposite extreme and nearly always make deceptive draws. With them, a two-card draw means that they have *not* got triplets. Note the mathematical players, and those who play by ear. Pick out the reckless gambler who cannot be bluffed but who will call anything, and the cautious, careful player who has to be coaxed into calling genuine bets but can easily be bluffed. Observe whether a player changes his game according to whether he is winning or losing—nearly everyone does, and not necessarily in the obvious way of being more dashing when winning and more cautious when losing. Finally, note who bluffs, and how often, and what kind of bluff he favors.

Vary Your Game

There is in most poker situations a right and a wrong technical play, and that is what this book is mainly about. But it is no use playing absolutely by the book. You would make things far too easy for a skillful opponent. You must vary your own game. Play sometimes against the odds. Raise sometimes on a hand that scarcely justifies it. Make a stupid call occasionally to give the impression that you are a hard man to bluff. Disguise the fact that your play is basically tight by sometimes taking an outrageous risk, but don't overdo it. The more you stick to correct technical play the better. Just vary your play sufficiently often to keep opponents guessing, so that they can never be quite sure what any of your actions really mean.

At Table Stakes an added complication is that you must watch the stacks of your opponents, for their size may influence your tactics. The player with a bigger stack than yours presents an obvious danger. You must be very sure of your ground before you raise him, for he may raise you back to the extent of all your chips.

Less obvious is the danger of the man with a smaller stack than yours. You can't bluff him out if his stack is much smaller than the size of the pot, for he is getting such good odds he will call if he thinks he's got any chance at all. And if a player's stack gets very small he may be willing to push it all out on fairly light grounds because there is no danger of a re-raise. By the same token, if you yourself are getting low in chips, you can "tap," i.e., bet your whole stack, on only a bare margin of superiority. It is often better to do this than try to eke out your few chips as long as possible by ultra-tight play.

2. BLUFFING

If you asked someone who knew little about poker what was the point of bluffing, he would probably say, "To win money on bad hands, I suppose." Yet this is not more than 50 per cent of the object. Just as important is to ensure that you win money on your good hands. Basically, the way to win at poker is to bet heavily on your good hands and not at all on your bad hands. But by itself this policy would get you nowhere, for opponents would simply drop whenever you raised if they knew you never bluffed. In other words, a bluff is part of a general policy rather than an isolated business proposition in its own right. Just the same, you naturally want some of your bluffs to succeed, so that when the balance is struck they will show a direct profit as well as an indirect one. Here are a few generalities that may be helpful:

1. Don't bluff too often. If you have more than three bluffs called in an evening, you are probably overdoing it. On the other hand, with only one bluff called you may well be bluffing less than the traffic can bear.

2. Make your bluffs conform in every way to your usual style of play. Play exactly as you would if you really held the hand you are pretending to hold. Any unusual size of bet, as well as any unusual expression or behavior, will arouse suspicion.

3. Stick mostly to modest bluffs designed to collect a small pot from the holder of two pairs or so. The average player holding triplets or better is apt to call any bet no matter how convincing the evidence that he is beaten. Ambitious bluffs against good hands are likely to succeed only against good players and are wasted on the others.

For example, "A" passes up opening a Jackpot but backs in later and draws one card, obviously to a straight or flush. The opener draws two cards to three Kings, fails to improve, and checks. "A," who has filled a flush, bets the size of the pot. The opener raises the size of the pot, hoping that "A" will fall for his bluff and reason that the opener has a full house or fours. Most players in "A's" position, however, would call.

4. All types of bluff should be tried from time to time but experience shows that some types are better than others. A player who has raised an opener will seldom yield to a bluff, as everyone will be a witness when the openers are shown. Bluffs after missing out on a straight or flush are mostly unsuccessful. Pat hand bluffs, preceded by the appropriate raise before the draw, are mostly successful. Obviously you must not overdo them, but make sure that for every genuine pat hand you hold, you make one pat hand bluff.

5. Choose your victim carefully. You might try to bluff a naturally tight player who has been refusing to call your genuine bets. Even if your bluff fails, you will have corrected an undesirable tendency on his part. Or you might try someone who has been making a lot of unsuccessful calls lately: He may well now take a pessimistic view of further calls. Or some heavy loser who has lost his nerve as well as his money. Big winners are traditionally supposed to be difficult to bluff, but this is not invariably true. Some players are prodigal with their chips when they are well ahead. Others, in the face of a mild bluff, are quite likely to drop, like tame old circus lions, full of food, who can be lightly baited with impunity.

In general, it is obviously best to bluff when you have only one serious opponent, but sometimes advantage can be taken of the threat of a one-card draw over your main opponent. Take the following example:

The game is a seven-handed Jackpot. "A," on the left of the dealer, passes. "B" opens with a pair of Jacks. "C" stays, and "A" also stays. "A" draws one card, "B," the opener, and "C" both draw three cards. "B" does not improve his pair of Jacks. What should "B" do?

If "B" checks he will lose the pot since "C" almost certainly has a pair of Kings or Aces. With less he would hardly have stayed with the pot opened under the guns. But a bluff has a fair chance of success. "C" has a double threat. Not only is there the possibility that "B" is not bluffing, there is also the danger of "A," the one-card draw. "A," who passed opening, was obviously drawing to a straight or flush, and he may have filled. In the circumstances, "C" may be unwilling to call "B's" bet, and providing "A" has not filled (and the chances are, after all, 4 to 1 against) "B" will collect. This kind of bluff is known as a "squeeze."

Is He Bluffing?

Whenever an opponent makes a bet, the question has to be asked, "Is he bluffing?" More often than not, in fact much more often than not, the right answer is, "No." This applies particularly in the following cases:

1. A bet made when several players are still in the game. This applies to most bets made before the draw, and to some after. Few players will bluff when there are more than two opponents who might call, and in general they are right.

2. A bet made after several raises and re-raises. These kinds of super bluff are rare. And in a small-limit game they would mostly be ridiculous, for the raise would be so small in relation to the size of the pot that the bluff could succeed only against a special type of calculating but unimaginative player.

3. A comparatively small bet. It looks as if the bettor is trying to coax you to call rather than drive you out.

A bluff is more likely in the following cases:

1. Where the bettor has shown some abnormal expression or behavior, indicating that he is not playing his normal game. This sort of giveaway is hardly likely to occur in a high-class poker game.

2. When the bet is larger than would appear natural in the circumstances. Any bet larger than the size of the pot in a Table Stakes game should be viewed with suspicion. However, there is always the possibility that the bettor may be double bluffing, particularly if he is a clever player who has lately been giving the impression of an inveterate bluffer.

3. A bet after a one-card draw. The owner of a busted straight or flush has a great temptation to try and retrieve the situation, and this is the most common of all bluffs.

Before coming to a definite conclusion you should ask yourself another question: "Am I, from the point of view of the bettor, a likely victim for a bluff?" If you have been refusing lately to call his bets when he must have known you had a fairly good hand, then he may well be trying a bluff now.

Naturally there will be many exceptions to the above rules. There can be bluff, double bluff and triple bluff, and it is impossible to tie the subject up neatly. As we said before, anybody can make sure he is never bluffed. That's easy. It is also the mark of a poor player—and, before long, a poor man.

3. BLUFF IN SMALL-LIMIT POKER

The large-limit player will say, probably with more than a touch of scorn, that a small limit makes bluff impossible and cuts the importance of psychology practically to zero. This overstates the case. It is true that in a small-limit game it is, or should be, impossible to win a big pot by a bluff. If the limit is 5 chips and the pot reaches 40 chips, few players would make the mistake of failing to call a further 5-chip raise. The percentages overwhelmingly favor a call in almost any circumstances. But in the small pots a bluff may well be worthwhile on occasions. A 5-chip bluff may stand to collect you 20 chips. Such a bluff need have only 1 chance in 4 of being successful to be an economic proposition. Of course you cannot estimate the chances of success with this degree of accuracy, but the point to remember is that the small-limit player can afford to have several failures for each successful bluff, whereas the large-limit player, usually betting the size of the pot, must see more than half his bluffs succeed in order to show a direct profit.

You cannot pull off a super bluff in small-limit poker, but the alert player can still find opportunities in the psychological field. He is helped by the fact that lengthy deliberation is not customary in this kind of game. A disinterested player will often surrender a small pot with very little thought.

4. TIGHT VERSUS LOOSE PLAY

This is a faintly embarrassing subject for all writers on poker. They, and we, are primarily concerned in trying to tell their readers how to win at poker. And to win at poker you must play tight. This means throwing in a lot of middling hands, which is dull for the player himself and tends to dampen down the whole game. This applies to all forms of poker, not just Jackpots. It is an awkward fact for the enthusiasts. A consequence is that when all the players in a game know their way around, they tend to look for variations where initiative is more rewarding.

Fortunately most people play poker for fun and, though they like to win, winning is not the sole object of the exercise. And so there is in many groups a compromise, unspoken and almost unrealized, that everyone will loosen up more or less to the same degree. Anyone who fails to conform will just not be asked to join in the game again. For these groups some of our advice will appear impracticable, and of course it should not be followed. If we joined that group we would not follow it ourselves. To tell the truth, that kind of poker can be more amusing than a game where everyone has tightened up desperately.

The foregoing applies mainly to small-limit games. At pot limit it is generally conceded that the object is to win and everyone is doing the best he can. The possibility of any pot's suddenly pyramiding to huge proportions is sufficient to keep the game tense even through a prolonged spell of uninteresting hands.

5. THE QUESTION OF LUCK

Luck, good and bad, is mostly mixed up in a haphazard jumble, and in the long run everyone can expect to have his fair share of both. But sometimes, as every card player knows, luck can run in one direction for an awfully long time. When this happens nearly everyone follows the natural instinct to play boldly when in luck and winning, and cautiously when out of luck and losing. In principle, there is nothing wrong in this, but nearly always it is overdone. There is no point in playing a promising hand feebly just because you are, or seem to be, out of luck. This will simply ensure that if you do get a lucky break you won't get the full benefit. Nor does it suddenly become sound tactics to play against the odds just because you are winning heavily, or you will fritter away your winnings very quickly when the luck turns.

It is only in the doubtful, borderline cases that it is right to follow your luck. It will often happen that you think you probably have the best hand but aren't quite certain that the margin of probability is sufficient for a raise. Then certainly it is entirely reasonable to play an aggressive game and raise when you are in a winning streak, and take a more pessimistic view and simply call when nothing seems to be going right.

There is, however, no scientific basis to justify this advice. In theory, the fact that you have had a steady run of vile luck, or of fantastically good luck, cannot have the slightest effect either way on what happens next. But in practice few card players will deny that luck does appear sometimes to have a distinct bias, and the sensible player will make reasonable, though not excessive, allowance for this. At any rate, he will recognize that when his luck is poor, so may be his judgment.

Very few people are totally unmoved by a prolonged spell of bad luck. The actual money involved may not matter, but the fact of losing will irritate them and so dull their perception. If the cash losses do mean something, the effect is aggravated. The unfortunate player may begin to play so cautiously that he deprives himself of any chance at all of reducing his losses and leaves himself wide open to bluff, or he may lose his head and start to plunge wildly and recklessly. Even if he is exceptionally levelheaded, he is, at the very least, unlikely to be doing himself real justice. Conversely, a winning player, provided he avoids the temptation of betting recklessly and against the odds, is at the top of his form: keen, clear thinking, quick to exploit every favorable opportunity.

There is, therefore, something to be said for stopping early when you are losing and playing until dawn when you are winning.

There is certainly nothing to be said for the opposite policy, which will simply ensure that you spend most of your time at the poker table playing below your true form. Yet curiously enough this is the policy that most people follow. How often has one seen a heavy loser striving frantically to prolong the game? And how often does this ever do anything but increase his losses!

6. THE QUALITIES OF A GOOD PLAYER

A summary of our advice up to now might read as follows:

1. Know the percentages and play to them except when you have a well-defined tactical reason for doing otherwise.

2. Be a bold bettor. When you think you have the best hand before the draw, make it as expensive as you can for opponents to stay with you. After the draw continue to keep opponents at full stretch. Remember that the percentages are always against —in many cases heavily against—a player's improving in the draw.

This advice is perhaps more suitable for the small-limit player than the large, but no one should regret losing money through betting up a good hand.

3. Bluff sufficiently often to ensure that you cash in on your winning hands. Remember that chips lost because your opponent has not seen your final bet are just as valuable as the same number lost in an unsuccessful bluff.

4. Irrespective of your hand, drop out of the game as soon as you think you are beaten, but when it comes to the final stage, pay to call rather than have doubts afterwards. (This advice applies less to a large-limit game, where the principle should rather be: Keep your feet on the ground and aim to be on the right side whenever you become involved for big money.)

5. Play your players, noting not only how they play in general, but what sort of a mood they are in. So far as possible, stay clear of a big winner. We say that, not from a superstitious belief that the luck will continue, but because such players are hard to gauge. It is a little like starting an argument with a drunk, who is liberated from the normal restraints.

These are the main principles of good play, but there is rather more to being a good player. Almost the only invariable rule in poker is that you should never do anything consistently. You must vary your game to include every stratagem we have mentioned, good or bad. In addition to being unpredictable, you must be inscrutable.

CHAPTER FOUR

STRAIGHT DRAW POKER

Straight Draw Poker means simply the basic form of Draw Poker, without any opening requirements or other embellishments. It is played less often than Jackpots, though for five players it is really a better game. Five-handed Jackpots are won all too often by the opener, and also entail a fair number of re-deals because no one can open.

1. ANYTHING OPENS

The game requires a very similar technique to Jackpots, the only difference being that there is far more sandbagging, i.e., declining to open with a strong hand in order to raise the eventual opener. This means that even a middle opener, say the third or fourth to act, is really under the guns and should exercise due caution.

In a seven-handed game the first, second and even third to act should not open—whatever their hands are. If you have a fair hand, there is no point in getting committed until the situation is clearer. If you have an excellent hand, there is no point in playing it from the unfavorable position of the opener. In this game, unlike Jackpots, there is little danger that everyone will drop out. Someone nearly always opens.

In the middle positions, to open for a real bet you need a pair of Kings in a seven-handed game, a pair of Queens in a six-handed game, and a pair of Jacks in a five-handed game. The last two to act can open on a pair of Jacks or a pair of tens, respectively. There is no harm for any late player to open for a chip or two with a four-card straight or flush, just to see what happens. If sometimes in this position he makes a small opening bet with a really strong hand in order to attract competition, he will keep opponents guessing when he opens for a small amount.

Playing against the opener, play normally as though it were an ordinary Jackpot. However, a late opener may well have only a moderate pair or even a four-card straight or flush, and you can drop your standards slightly for staying and raising. There may be sandbaggers around, but on the whole, it looks as if the opposition is weak.

After the draw the play is similar to Jackpots. However, there may be less information about the opposing hands, for the fact that a player did not open does not necessarily mean his hand was not good enough to do so. It is also not so easy as in Jackpots to distinguish between one-card draws to two pairs and one-card draws to a flush or straight.

2. PASS OUT

This is an alternative way of playing Straight Draw Poker. The only difference is that you can't pass and then back in later if someone else opens. You must either open or drop out of the game and throw in your hand. If no one opens, the dealer collects the antes.

Opening

The first to act, on the immediate left of the dealer, is in the worst position. If the game is seven-handed, there are six players sitting over him who may raise. He requires an extra margin of strength and should not open with less than a pair of Kings, at least not in a large-limit game. If first to act passes out, second to act is in a slightly better position in that he has only five potential opponents who may raise. He needs slightly less strength, and can open with a pair of Queens.

As each player in turn passes out, the next one is in a progressively better position, and his requirements for opening drop. Third to act needs a pair of Jacks, and subsequent players can open on any medium pair. Finally we come to the last-but-one to act, with the dealer as his only possible opponent. The chances are slightly against the dealer's having even a pair, and last-but-one to act can open with an Ace, King or any pair, however small.

In a six-handed game, first to act corresponds to second to act in the above paragraphs and would need a pair of Queens to open; second to act would need Jacks. In a five-handed game first to act needs a pair of Jacks.

The normal opening bet would be the size of the pot (if the limit allows). If you have slightly less than the suggested minimum, you can occasionally open for a smaller amount. This probably won't do you much good in that particular hand, but later on you may want to open deceptively for a small amount with a rockcrusher. In that case your previous play may make this a less obvious bit of sandbagging.

In a small-limit game you get a much better percentage on your opening bet, and opening requirements can be dropped to a high pair for an early opener and any pair for middle and late opener.

Staying and Raising before the Draw

If opponents keep roughly to the opening table, due allowance must be made when playing against the opener. He should be credited with holding rather more than the minimum requirements for his position. Stay, then, if you are probably equal to the opener, and raise if you are better. For players used to playing draw in the form of Jackpots, it may seem unnatural to raise with only a pair, but in Pass Out this is often the right play. An early opener will probably have a very high pair and should certainly not be raised with less than two pairs, or two pairs of nines up in a large-limit game. But a middle opener, say fourth or fifth to act in a seven-handed game, will open (if he is playing correctly) with a medium pair, and on average will have around Jacks or

Queens. Play, therefore, with a pair of Jacks, and raise with a pair of Aces. Last-but-one to act will certainly open with any pair, or even an Ace, King. Therefore you should stay with any pair, and raise with a pair of tens.

Many players are constitutionally incapable of raising with only a pair and, in general, raises before the draw in this game should be given about the same face value as they have in Jackpots or Straight Draw Poker where checking and backing in is allowed. This means roughly that the first raise indicates two pairs, the second raise three of a kind, the third a pat straight or flush, the fourth a full house, the fifth fours.

Whether Straight Draw Poker should be played "back in" or "pass out" is open to argument. Actually, it is played more often under "back in" rules, perhaps because this provides a more open game. On the other hand, the game then becomes so similar to Jackpots that it is somewhat pointless to play it. The Pass Out game, in its early stages at any rate, does bring new factors into play.

3. BLIND AND STRADDLE

This is the original form of Draw Poker, but it began to lose popularity with the introduction of Jackpots. Today it has gone out of fashion in the U.S., though oddly enough, it still remains the basic draw game in England, Australia and South Africa.

The game is played as follows: The player on the left of the dealer, who is called the *blind*, before looking at his cards puts up an ante of 1 chip. The player on his left, known as the *straddle*, puts up an ante of 2 chips. The third player from the dealer is first to act. He has the choice of opening for 4 chips—he cannot bet either more or less than this—or passing out and throwing in his hand. If he passes out, the player on his left has the same choice, opening for 4 chips or passing out. If everyone passes before the blind, the blind is only required to bet 3 chips on top of his 1-chip ante. If the blind passes, the straddle collects the 1 chip from the blind and his own 2-chip ante, and the deal passes for the next hand.

If someone opens, the game proceeds in the usual way, each subsequent player having the choice of passing, staying or raising. When it comes to the blind and straddle, who have already contributed 1 chip and 2 chips respectively, these chips are counted as part of any bet they may now choose to make. For instance, if an earlier player has already made the opening bet of 4 chips, and no one has raised, the blind may stay for only a further 3 chips, and the straddle for only a further 2 chips.

The game is sometimes played with the straddle optional. If the second player decides not to straddle, he becomes first to act after looking at his cards. In this case, he can open for twice the blind, i.e., 2 chips. Sometimes re-straddling is allowed by the third player from the dealer, so that the blinds become 1, 2, and 4 chips. In this case, the fourth player becomes first to act. He must bet twice the re-straddle, i.e., 8 chips, or pass.

The advantage of straddling or re-straddling when it is optional is that you play the hand from the best position—the last to speak. The disadvantage is that you are obliged to stake chips on a hand which may be worthless. In practice, most people don't weigh up the pros and cons carefully, but simply straddle if they want to boost up the stakes. A player who re-straddles when others are not doing so at their turn may have a lucky run, but theoretically he is at a disadvantage.

Opening

If there is one straddle there will be 3 chips in antes, and the opening player must bet 4 chips if he wants to play. It follows that you should not bet these 4 chips unless you reckon that you have a slightly better than even chance of winning the pot against all opposition. Naturally, as in Pass Out, it makes a great difference how many players there are to follow. Suppose that you are first to speak in a seven-handed game: Unless you have a pair of Aces or better you are not entitled to think that yours is the best hand.

But suppose you are the dealer and that the first four have thrown in: then there are only two players to follow, and if you have a medium pair such as eights, it is even money that yours will be the best of the three remaining hands.

Using this mathematical basis, the conventional requirements for opening the betting in a seven-handed game are as follows:

If first to act	A pair of Aces
If second to act	A pair of Kings
If third to act	A pair of Queens
If fourth to act	A pair of tens
If fifth to act	A pair of eights
If sixth to act	Ace, King.

You will note that the ante or blind can play on any pair, on an Ace, King, and indeed on a hope, such as one to a flush. It costs him only 3 chips to play (in addition to the 1 he has already contributed), so he is getting even money. The odds are slightly against the last player having a playable hand of any kind, so as often as not in these circumstances the hand will be won without competition.

The table above is of ancient vintage and was, as a matter of fact, devised by the old-time professional gamblers when straddling was rare and the opener was mostly betting 2 chips over a 1 chip ante. Thus it by no means deserves unquestioning respect. There is, for instance, very little difference at this stage between Aces and Kings, while in the later stages to make much difference between the middle pairs is artificial.

Most good players are "ante snatchers." That is to say, when they are playing in reasonable form and the opponents on their left are not greatly to be feared, they will often, in the later positions, make plays that are not theoretically justified.

The worst mistake in this phase of the game is to lower unduly the requirements in first and second position. To play regularly on a pair of Queens in first position is bad mathematically and possesses neither tactical nor psychological compensation. Much better is to play only on Aces or Kings on principle and occasionally to play on a low pair and perhaps draw two cards.

In a five-handed game the first to act will be in the same position as third to act in the table above. Thus, if he plays strictly according to standard, he will need a pair of Queens to open. The second player will need a pair of tens, and so on.

Staying and Raising

The technique here is similar to Pass Out after a pot-sized opening bet. Apart from the ante and the blind, anyone who plays against the opener alone is getting only 7 to 4 for his money. Since the odds against beating a better hand are practically never less than 3 to 1 (the exception being when you draw to an open-ended straight flush), it is a losing proposition in the long run to stay with a hand inferior to the opener's. If your opponents stick more or less to the opening table, you must take into account that on the average the opener will hold rather better than the precise minimum for his position. If you can equal this, stay. If you can better it, raise. This means that against an early opener you can stay with a pair of Aces and raise with a good two pairs, say Queens up. (Low two pairs are a doubtful proposition in these circumstances, on the whole a less promising holding than a pair of Aces.) If a middle player opens, stay with a pair of Queens, and raise with a pair of Aces or any two pairs. The straddle, having better odds to his money, can stay on a low pair against a late player.

The straddle against the ante is one of the most critical encounters in this game. In about one third of the hands played, the early players will pass. Thus a player's fortunes will depend to a large extent on how he conducts this final battle. The ante, if a reasonably aggressive player, will attempt to snatch the blind on any pair and sometimes even without a pair. It follows that if, as the straddle, you have as good as a pair of Jacks, you probably have the best hand and should raise. You can stay with any pair or Ace, King or a four-card straight or flush.

So far we have assumed no active players except the opener. But of course it will also happen, though not so often as in Jackpots, that one or more other players will have stayed in front of you.

As more players stay, you naturally have better odds to your money, but on most types of hand your chances of winning will decrease at a steeper rate. You should, therefore, be less inclined to tangle with two or more opponents than with one, and standards for staying and raising should be adjusted upwards. The exception is with four-card straights and flushes. Against the opener alone, only the straddle is justified in playing with either of these holdings. With one other player besides the opener, the blind can stay with a four flush, and with three players already in the hand, anyone can play with a four flush, and it wouldn't be far wrong to play with a bobtail straight.

The Draw and After

This game does not produce any problems here that have not been discussed already.

PROBLEMS AND ANSWERS

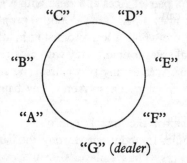

"C"   "D"

"B"   "E"

"A"   "F"

"G" (*dealer*)

Problem 1. The game is straight draw, back in. "A," "B" and "C" pass. What should "D" do with a pair of Jacks?

Answer. Owing to the danger of sandbagging by one of the early players, "D's" hand is not good enough for a sizable opening bet in a seven-handed game. "D" should pass, and await events.

Problem 2. The game is Pass Out. "A" and "B" have passed out. What should "C" do with a pair of Jacks?

Answer. "C" should open for the limit up to the size of the pot. He probably has the best hand, but he doesn't want the short pairs to come in cheaply.

Problem 3. The game is Pass Out. "F" opens, everyone before him having passed. What should "G" do with a pair of tens?

Answer. "F" would open with any pair, and possibly with only an Ace. "G" probably has the better hand and should therefore raise. (If the game were pot limit, "G" would require a pair of Jacks to raise.)

Problem 4. The game is the classical form of Straight Draw, Blind and Straddle. "A" is the blind. "B" has straddled. "C" makes the opening bet of 4 chips. "D," "E" and "F" drop, but "G" stays. What should "A" do with ♣ J ◇ J 6 2 A?

Answer. "A's" pair of Jacks is useless. Probably both "C" and "G" have higher pairs. But the odds in chips are just good enough for "A" to play his four flush. There are 11 chips in the pot and he can stay for 3 chips. The exact odds against his filling his flush are just over 4 to 1, but he should accept 11 to 3 because, if he improves, he can raise after the draw with good prospects of winning.

Problem 5. The same game as above. "A" is the blind, "B" has straddled. This time "E" makes the opening bet. What should "A" do with the same ♣ J ◇ J 6 2 A?

Answer. This time "A" should play his pair of Jacks, which has a fair chance of being higher than "E's" pair. The odds in chips of 7 to 3 do not justify "A's" playing a four flush.

CHAPTER FIVE

LOWBALL

Lowball, almost unknown before the Second World War, is now a regular feature of almost every poker game anywhere in the world. In England, it is called Misère.

In Lowball, the value of the cards is reversed. That is to say, the lowest hand wins the pot. A variation from normal, too, is that Aces count low. Playing that version of Lowball, when you drew one card to 2 3 4 6, you would hope for an Ace. This, provided the hand is not a flush, would give you a cinch, an unbeatable hand, A 2 3 4 6. If you were to draw a 7 or an 8, that would still be a fair hand in Lowball. A 5 would be a straight and, in effect, a disaster.

Lowball has a lesser element of calculation than the games described in the previous chapters, and so is rather easier to play. It produces plenty of action, particularly in a small-limit game. It can also be played with enjoyment by fewer than five players.

1. PERCENTAGES

The average winning hand in this game is in the region of a good nine high, such as 9 7 5 3 2, or a moderate eight high, such as 8 7 5 4 A. However, many pots are won by much worse (i.e., ordinarily much better) hands, for when two or more players are all drawing cards, all may end up with a pair.

The following table will give you an idea of the frequency with which you may expect to hold a passable pat hand.

Odds against being dealt:

A pat cinch (6 4 3 2 A)	2,540 to 1
A pat six high	635 to 1
A pat seven high	180 to 1
A pat eight high	75 to 1
A pat nine high	35 to 1
A pat ten high	20 to 1

More important than any of these individual odds is to know that it is 20 to 1 against being dealt a pat nine high or lower (a different chance, of course, from a pat nine high precisely), and about 9 to 4 against anyone's holding such a hand in a seven-handed game. A pat ten high, though shown in the table, is seldom worth playing.

Also important is the fact that in a seven-handed game the chances are that at least one player has four cards not higher than an eight. As we shall see, competition in this game is usually restricted to pat hands and one-card draws. About half the hands dealt are three cards to an eight, but two-card draws have roughly the same value in Lowball as short pairs in a Jackpot. They can sometimes be played in a small-limit game when the conditions are right, but not very often in a large-limit game, at least not if it is seven-handed.

The odds against improving (assuming that you have a hand that will not readily decline into a straight or flush) are:

Drawing one card, it is:

    Evens against finishing ten high or lower

    11 to 8 against finishing nine high or lower

    2 to 1 against finishing eight high or lower

    3 to 1 against finishing seven high or lower

    5 to 1 against finishing six high

Drawing two cards, it is:

    6 to 4 against finishing Jack high or lower

    9 to 4 against finishing ten high or lower

    7 to 2 against finishing nine high or lower

    6 to 1 against finishing eight high or lower

    10 to 1 against finishing seven high or lower

Knowledge of these odds is useful at the time of the draw and in the later betting, particularly when you have only one opponent.

The chances of beating the opener cannot be stated with great exactitude as standards for opening may vary. But as a general guide, if you assume the opener to hold on the average something between a pat nine and a one-card draw to an eight, you can say that drawing one to a good eight, the odds are slightly against you; drawing one to a good seven, about even; drawing two cards to a seven, about 3 to 1 against you.

2. BEFORE THE DRAW

Opening

The normal standard for opening is a pat nine high, such as 9 8 6 4 A, or a one-card draw to an eight high, such as K 8 7 4 3. It is not good policy to open on less in most Lowball games, though in a small-limit, five-handed game a hand such as 10 9 6 4 2 is a possibility if everyone else has passed. If you finish up with one opponent, your ten high has about an even-money chance of standing up after the draw. If you have more than one opponent, draw two cards to the six and hope for the best.

In a seven-handed game, sandbagging in the early positions is quite common.

Staying and Raising

Subject to the usual rule that rather more strength is required when there are still several players to follow, this is how the various types of hands should be played after the pot has been opened:

(a) *Pat hands*

10 9 7 6 5. A pat ten high is not an attractive hand. It should be played only in the most favorable circumstances, far around the table and with the opener as your only opponent.

9 8 6 4 3. A pat nine high is a good hand to pick up at the deal but, rather like two pairs in Draw Poker, it probably won't stand

up after the draw if you have more than one or two opponents. Therefore the normal rule is to make a protective raise with the objective of keeping down the number of competitors.

8 7 5 3 2. A pat eight high is always worth a raise, and in most cases a re-raise. A pat seven high is worth a third raise, and a pat six high a fourth raise.

(b) One-card draws

K 9 8 6 4. A one-card draw to a nine high is not a good proposition.

J 8 7 4 3. Stay with this one-card draw to an eight high. But not with J 8 7 6 5. It is rarely a good proposition to stay on any bobtail straight, whether headed by 8, 7, 6 or 5.

K 7 5 3 A. A one-card draw to a good seven high, that is, 7 5 and no possibility of ending up with a straight or flush, is worth a raise before the draw, especially when there are two or three players already in the pot.

(c) Two-card draws

Just as the Draw Poker player is taught at his mother's knee the maxim, "Don't play a short pair," the Lowball player is taught, "Don't make two-card draws." This may well be good advice for a large-limit game, but the small-limit player can quite often stay with a two-card draw to a seven high without losing a percentage. For instance, if the ante is 14 chips, and the pot is opened for the limit of 5 chips, you can take a chance with K J 7 3 A unless you are next to the opener and in danger of a raise from any of the remaining players.

Even the large-limit player may well have to make an occasional two-card draw, if only to keep himself from becoming too unpopular.

The odds never favor drawing three cards.

To sum up the betting before the draw, as a rough guide the opener usually has a one-card draw to an eight but may have a pat nine high. First raise suggests a pat nine high or one-card draw to a seven, a second raise suggests a pat eight high, and a third raise a pat seven high.

3. PROBLEMS IN THE DRAW

These are the sorts of hands that present a problem in the draw:

9 8 6 3 A. Once in, you should normally take your chance on the pat nine high. If the indications are that there is a good pat hand against you, then two cards to the 6 would represent a rather better proposition than one to the 8 6.

9 7 5 4 2. Here you can break up the nine high and draw one to a good seven, but you would have to be very sure of your ground before doing so. For the most part, stand on the pat nine high.

7 6 5 4 3. In this exasperating situation, and others like it, the card to throw, if you play at all, is the one next to the top. An exception is 5 4 3 2 A, when you should discard the 5 rather than the 4.

Against One Opponent

The right draw can be different against a single opponent, especially when he draws first. Against an opponent who draws two cards you should stand on a Jack high, for it is 6 to 4 against his making as good a hand. Against an opponent who draws one card you should stand on a ten, whether good or bad.

4. BETTING AFTER THE DRAW

An eight high is worth a raise in most positions, and a seven high a re-raise. A six high is normally worth a third raise, but a bad six, headed by 6 5 4, should not be rated higher than, say, a medium full house in Draw Poker. If it is beaten you can be disappointed but not amazed. Cinches, 6 4 3 2 A, are by no means unknown in Lowball.

Inevitably there is a fair amount of bluffing after the draw. A player who has made a hopeless hand such as a straight or medium pair will often try a bluff, at any rate in a small field, since he knows that if he checks he cannot possibly win. It is hard to call such a bet when you have drawn a pair oneself. Nevertheless, it is worth noting that, against an opponent who has drawn one card and raised, a pair of deuces will win nearly as often as a ten high, since with a hand in between those two the opener will usually check.

Against One Opponent

The standards for raising are quite different when there are only two active players, both drawing cards. When a player draws one card, the odds are even that he will not finish with better than ten high. If you make a fair nine high and are first to act, you should not check and allow your opponent a cheap showdown. Similarly, if you are second to act, and the first player has checked, nine high will win unless he is aiming to trap you, and in general you should take this risk and raise.

If your opponent has drawn two cards, it is 6 to 4 against his finishing Jack high or better. Once again, if you yourself make a Jack high you probably have the best hand, and should therefore raise. In a tight large-limit game these tactics may have to be applied with a little discretion, but it is in these sharp exchanges after the draw in Lowball that the good player has his main advantage.

5. CALIFORNIA LOWBALL

California Lowball is generally played with the additional rule that straights and flushes do not count. This makes 5 4 3 2 A the best hand. In this game, obviously, all the good hands mentioned in the previous pages become relatively a little less formidable. A pat seven high comes nearer to a pat eight high in ordinary Lowball, and so on.

6. LOWBALL PASS OUT

Lowball is sometimes played under pass out rules—you must either open or pass out, and cannot check. In England, it is often played with Blind and Straddle. If the former game is pot limit, the two games are essentially the same so far as tactics are concerned, so we can deal with them together.

Opening

The principle is that as each player drops out of the game, the next player can drop his minimum requirements for opening. The early players are roughly in the same position as the opener in an ordinary Lowball pot. They require at least a pat nine high or a one-card draw to an eight. A middle player, with only two or three possible opponents, can open with a pat ten high and possibly a two-card draw to a six. A later player, with only one or two possible opponents, can open with a pat Jack high or any two-card draw to an eight or better.

Staying and Raising

Against an early opener you require a one-card draw to an eight to stay. With a pat nine high, and possibly a one-card draw to a good seven, you can raise. Against a middle opener you can stay with a pat ten high, and raise with a pat nine high or any one-card draw to a seven. If you are last to speak and the opener is on your immediate right, the chances are he has no better than a two-card draw. Stay with a pat Jack high or any two-card draw to an eight. Raise with a pat ten high or a one-card draw to an eight.

The rest of the game, the draw and the end betting, does not present any new problems.

PROBLEMS AND ANSWERS

Problem 1. "A" opens. "B" stays with Q 8 4 3 A in different suits. "A" stands pat. "B" discards the Queen and draws a 6. "A" checks. What should "B" do?

Answer. "B" should bet. The chances are that "A" has a worse hand, probably a nine high. He will probably call even so, for players who have opened the pot are wary of a bluff in this situation.

Problem 2. "A" opens. "B" stays with Q 8 4 3 A in different suits. "C" also stays. Everybody draws one card, "B" getting a 6. "A" checks. What should "B" do?

Answer. "B" should also check. Against 2 one-card draws an 8 6 is not good enough for a bet. If "C" bets, "B" is good enough to call.

Problem 3. "A" opens. "B" stays. "C" stays with 10 9 6 3 A. "A" and "B" draw one card. What should "C" do?

Answer. "C" should draw two cards to the 6. His ten high has little chance of standing up against two one-card draws. Also, when the decision is at all close, it is generally right to play for a good hand that will inspire some confidence in the end betting.

CHAPTER SIX

DRAW POKER WITH THE BUG

This is a variation which is gaining in popularity. One joker, known as the "Bug," is added to the deck (in this case, the joker that comes with the deck) but it is a joker with limited powers. It can only be used as an Ace or to complete a straight or flush. In the case of equal hands, the usual rules apply, the Bug being given the value of the card it represents. For example, Bug ◇ A 10 4 3 would beat ♣ A Q 9 6 5 since the Bug in the first hand counts as a King. If the Bug is the only way of distinguishing between two hands, for instance B 9 7 6 5 in different suits against a natural straight to a nine, some games rule that the natural hand wins, others that the two hands divide the pot. It is possible, though extremely rare, to get five Aces in this game. This hand would beat a straight flush if it ever met one.

The Bug livens up the betting quite a bit by producing more playable one-card draws and more good hands in general. The incidence of straights is more than doubled. Yet it doesn't completely alter the character of the game. Three of a kind still remains a strong hand, good enough to win the majority of pots.

Play of Pairs

With a natural pair, opening and staying requirements are about the same as in Jackpots played with the normal deck of 52 cards. A pair lower than Aces is perhaps a shade weaker hand, but a low pair with an Ace or Bug kicker is quite a legitimate two-card draw.

The Bug and an Ace is a good hand, worth a raise before the draw. You have a 1 in 3 chance of improving two pairs to Aces up or better, 1 in 5 of getting three Aces. And you may just win unimproved. The normal draw is, of course, three cards. But if one of the odd cards could form part of a straight flush with your Ace, keep it and draw two cards. However, break up any straight combination, even B ♣ A ♡ K ◇ Q, and draw to the Bug Ace.

There is no percentage in drawing four cards to the Bug.

Play of Two Pairs and Triplets

The play of these hands is also unchanged in principle, always with the proviso that Aces up or three Aces are rather better hands, and lesser two pairs or triplets rather weaker hands. However, in most circumstances, two pairs is still worth a protective raise before the draw, and three of a kind is certainly worth one raise, and mostly a re-raise.

Don't be overawed by the Bug against you before the draw. Pat straights and flushes are still uncommon hands. You may well have a four-card straight or flush against you, but it is to your advantage to raise such a hand. You may drive him out, and even if you don't, the chances are he won't outdraw you. On the average you can reckon that if you don't hold the Bug yourself, a one-card draw by an opponent will fill about 1 in 3 times.

After the draw, three of a kind must generally be played with some caution. You will find yourself betting into a one-card draw pretty often, and the best thing to do is to check. If you bet, the one-card draw won't call if he hasn't filled, and if he has he will raise.

If you have been lucky enough to improve your two pairs or triplets into a full house or four of a kind, the Bug against you is more likely to increase your winnings than cost you the pot.

Play of Four-Card Straight Flushes

With an open-ended sequence and the Bug, such as B ◇ 5 6 7, you have a perfect combination that gives you nearly an even money chance (22 in 47 to be precise) of making a straight or better. This hand is worth a raise before the draw.

With B ♣ K Q J or B ♡ 4 3 2 or B ♠ 10 9 7, which are just short of the perfect combination, you have 2 chances in 5 of making a straight or better. Raise provided one other player besides the opener has stayed.

With a closed straight such as B ♢ A Q K or B ♣ 3 2 A, you have better than 1 chance in 3 of making a straight or better and, in addition, 1 chance in 16 of making three Aces. Besides this you may even collect the pot on a pair of Aces. This hand is also just worth a raise against the opener and one other player.

Even the worst combination of inside straight, B ♡ 5 7 9 or B ♣ 5 6 9, gives a 1 in 3 chance of a straight or better, and is always worth a raise against three opponents who have stayed.

Play of Four-Card Straights

Four-card straights are not quite good enough for an opening bet but they are usually worth playing.

With the Bug and an open-ended, three-card sequence such as B ♣ 5 ♢ 6 ♡ 7, you have a very fair hand. It will fill 1 in 3 times, and is therefore always worth playing.

With B K Q J or B 4 3 2 or B 5 6 8 in different suits, you have slightly less chance of improving, 1 in 4 to be exact. To stay with any of these hands you need odds in chips of 3 to 1, which in practice will often be obtainable.

The worst kind of inside straight, such as B 5 7 9 or B 5 8 9 in different suits, or a natural four-card straight, is a more doubtful proposition. You want odds in chips of 5 to 1, which you may sometimes get in a small-limit game but not often in a large one.

As already mentioned, B A K Q or B A 2 3 in different suits are best played as a three-card draw to the Bug Ace.

Play of Four-Card Flushes

An ordinary four flush, with or without the Bug, has about the same value as in Draw Poker with the normal 52 card deck. It is not worth an opening bet, and to play it at all you need odds in chips of 4 to 1.

If the hand is a four flush and also contains the Bug and an Ace, then your prospects are very fair. You will improve to two pairs Aces up or better rather more than 1 in 3 times, and you may even win the pot on your two Aces. This hand is worth an opening bet. If there are several players who have stayed, you can take a chance and raise in a small-limit game.

A hand like B ◇ A 10 3 ♣ 3 presents some problems. It can be treated as two pairs Aces up or as a four flush in diamonds. Generally it is best to treat it as two pairs Aces up, which stands a good chance of winning the average pot without improvement. But if the betting has indicated triplets elsewhere, it is best to take the 1 in 5 chance of filling the flush rather than the 1 in 10 chance of getting a full house.

Two-Card Draws

There is no percentage in making two-card draws to straights or flushes, and the only three-card straight flushes worth playing are the Bug and two adjacent or nearly adjacent cards, such as B ◇ 6 7 or B ♣ 6 8. However, as already mentioned, if one card in the sequence is an Ace then the other card should be retained and only two cards drawn. With B ◇ A 5 ♣ Q ♡ 8, discard the Queen and the eight.

In case this advice seems complicated, here is a summary of the play of straights and flushes:

1. A four-card straight flush including the Bug is a good hand, worth a raise before the draw in most circumstances.

2. A four-card straight including the Bug is not normally good enough for an opening bet, but unless it is an inside straight with two missing cards it is usually correct to stay.

3. Four-card flushes with or without the Bug, natural open-ended straights, and four-card inside straights with the Bug, are worth playing only if you are getting attractive odds in chips, 4 to 1 in the case of the flush, otherwise 5 to 1.

4. The only two-card draw that is legitimate is two cards to B ♠ 6 7 or B ◇ 7 9, or similar combinations.

CHAPTER SEVEN

DEUCES WILD

This is Draw Poker with all deuces wild, i.e., jokers that can be used to represent any card in the pack. A joker is considered as exactly equal to the card it represents. K 2 2 10 6 would beat K K K 8 7 by virtue of the 10 beating the 8. Five of a kind is a possible hand and ranks above a straight flush.

The game is often not taken very seriously in America, but in England, where it is called a freak pot, it is a regular feature of most poker sessions. It is in fact a good game which requires a high degree of technical skill to play properly.

The original object of introducing four jokers was to stir up the betting, and the percentages do in fact favor more players coming into the pot than into a Jackpot. The whole level of hands is considerably raised, the incidence of triplets, straights and four of a kind being particularly increased. The average opening hand is middle triplets and the average winning hand three Aces. Players accustomed to a game without wild cards at first tend to bet more freely than their hands warrant, but if they play the variation regularly they soon adjust themselves to the new conditions.

1. OPENING

Reasonable standards are as follows:

In the early positions, under the guns: 10 10 2 or any better hand containing a joker. So far as chances of improvement go, 10 10 10 is the same as 10 10 2, but when you have no joker you should generally wait for someone else to open. There is obviously an increased possibility of good hands against you, and you don't want to run into raises before the draw with any natural hand lower than a full house.

In the middle positions: Any triplets including a joker or a natural hand of A A A, or better. A natural straight, incapable of improvement, is not such a good hand as three Aces, and here again it may be better to wait. An open or semi-open straight containing a joker, for instance 2 6 7 8 or 2 6 7 9, or any four cards which could develop into a straight flush, is a fair opening hand. A joker and an Ace is borderline.

In the later positions: A joker and four odd cards, or a natural pair of Aces, or natural triplets, or better. If you are last to speak and no one has opened, there is a reasonable presumption that there are jokers waiting to be drawn.

In a large-limit game you might have to raise these standards slightly. In the later positions, with a very good hand such as four of a kind or two jokers, you may consider sandbagging with an opening bet of one or two chips, masking this play by sometimes making a small opening bet with an indifferent hand. It will be appreciated that with two jokers in your own hand the opposing hands are likely to be weak, and a limit opening bet may keep everyone out.

2. THE ODDS AGAINST IMPROVEMENT

The odds against improving various classes of hands not only affect the decision whether to stay or raise (in this game one quite often raises on prospects), but they also sometimes affect the draw. These are the odds relating to the more common holdings:

Drawing four cards to a joker:

2 to 1 against triplets.

4 to 1 against a straight or better.

If this hand does improve to better than triplets, it will generally be to either a straight or four of a kind, rarely to a flush, full house or five of a kind.

Drawing two cards to triplets:

5 to 1 against a full house or better.

You are much more likely, here, to make four of a kind than a full house.

Drawing three cards to two jokers:

6 to 4 against a straight or better.

4 to 1 against four of a kind.

The poorest hand you can make is three eights.

As to one-card draws, the flexibility of the joker, as in Draw Poker with the Bug, makes it easier to fill a straight than a flush. The odds in this case are:

11 to 10 on making a flush or straight from 2 ◇ 6 7 8.

6 to 1   against making a straight flush from the above hand.

15 to 10 against making a straight from 2 6 7 8 in different suits.

2 to 1   against making a straight from 2 6 7 9 in different suits.

16 to 10 against making a straight or better from ◇ 6 7 8 9.

7 to 1   against making a straight flush from the above hand.

3 to 1   against making a flush from ♣ 6 7 9 K or 2 ♡ 6 7 K.

It is not necessary to remember these odds in detail, but it is wise to look at them to check whether you have any false notions.

3. PLAYING AGAINST THE OPENER

If we assume that the opener has middle triplets on the average, your chances of beating him are as follows:

Drawing to	2 8 8	even
	2 ◇ 6 7 8	even
	2 6 7 8	2 to 1 against
	2	3 to 1 against
	2 6 8 9	3 to 1 against
	2 ♠ 6 9 K	4 to 1 against
	◇ 3 6 9 K	4 to 1 against

What is significant in this table is that drawing four cards to a joker presents about the same chance as drawing one card to an inside straight or to a flush. Tactical considerations affecting this choice are examined in a later section.

Bearing in mind that you always need to be somewhat stronger than minimum if the pot has been opened under the guns, and can be somewhat weaker if the limit prevents the opener from betting something approaching the size of the total ante, you can assess your hand as follows:

Natural triplets, short of three Aces. Low triplets are a doubtful proposition except possibly against a late opener. High triplets are usually just worth playing.

Natural three Aces. This hand is worth a protective raise before the draw, especially if the pot has not been opened under the guns.

Natural straight. Worth a protective raise. Even if several players have stayed you can take a chance on a raise. Unlike Draw Poker with a normal pack, in this game a large number of competitors indicates that the jokers may be well distributed and that the winning hand may not have to be a very good one.

Natural flush. This hand is also worth a raise, for the same reasons.

Triplets including a joker. Stay in any position. With 2 A A, raise.

Joker and four odd cards. Just worth staying, except in unfavorable position, next to an early opener.

Two jokers. This is a very promising hand indeed, but with half the jokers in your own hand opposing hands may be weak, and you don't want to scare them out. If near to the opener, simply stay. Further around the table, raise.

The following hands are generally not worth playing:

One-card draw to a natural straight or flush. The odds against filling are better than in Draw Poker with the normal pack, but the hand is by no means so certain to win.

A A. This hand is worth playing only in a favorable position such as last to speak against one opponent. Then there is a fair chance that you will draw one or two jokers.

Two pairs Aces up. No better than a pair of Aces, for you would draw three cards.

In general, before the draw, one raise suggests a pat straight or two jokers, a second raise a high pat flush, a third raise four of a kind.

4. PROBLEMS IN THE DRAW

The best draw is not always obvious in this game. The problems arise on hands that contain either one or two jokers.

As noted in the last section, drawing four cards to a joker presents about the same chance of beating the average opener as drawing one card to a semi-open straight or flush. As a rule the four-card draw should be preferred because then you have a chance of making a really good hand on which you can bet with some enthusiasm after the draw. But against one opponent who has drawn two cards, draw to the straight.

Faced with the choice of drawing one card to a straight or flush, prefer the straight if it is open or semi-open, as you have a better chance of filling. But suppose you hold 2 ♠ 5 7 10 ◇ 6 and two opponents have each drawn one card. Now you must conclude they were drawing to straights or flushes (not to four of a kind as they did not raise) and your best chance is to draw to the spade flush rather than the low straight.

With a joker and four odd cards you should normally draw four cards. But keeping an odd Ace does no harm, especially if you have only one opponent and he has drawn two or three cards. It is also sound policy to draw two cards to a promising nucleus such as 2 ♣ K Q. Apart from numerous chances to make hands from a royal straight flush down to three Queens, you may, even if you miss out, win the pot by raising against opponents with no more than low triplets.

With two jokers and three odd cards, the normal draw should be three cards. But keep an odd Ace, since three Aces will often win a pot without improvement. And if you have four cards that look promising for a straight flush, draw one card; you still have your chance of making four of a kind. However it is a waste of two jokers to draw one card to a simple straight or flush.

Sometimes you will have a pat straight or flush that includes two jokers. Stand on this hand unless there is evidence that something better will be needed to win the pot. For example, with 2 2 6 9 10 in different suits, you would break up the poorish straight if an opponent had raised and stood pat.

The only other kind of hand that raises any problem is when you have pat four of a kind. If you have had the chance of raising before the draw, it is good play to stand pat on high four of a kind, abandoning the slight chance of making five of a kind, which in any case will probably not be needed. By standing pat you give the impression of having only a straight or flush and may lure an opponent into raising on a weaker hand.

5. END BETTING

The betting after the draw depends, naturally, very much on what has gone before. With only a couple of active players, neither having given much indication of strength, three Aces would be a fair raise. In a stronger field an early player should only check with a straight or flush. A later player could raise on such a hand if he had drawn cards, but it would be rash to raise if he had stood pat. The difference in this respect between a Jackpot and Deuces Wild is that in a Jackpot a pat hand might be a bluff and for that reason may get called by a weaker hand. But in Deuces Wild, where the chances of improving are much better, to stand pat as a bluff would be eccentric play.

It is also risky to raise on a straight or flush in front of a two-card draw. If this player re-raises—and it is only 3 to 1 against his improving—you will have a difficult decision whether or not to call, for this is a situation in which a bluff is not uncommon. Even more dangerous is an opponent who has raised and drawn one card, and may well hold four of a kind, or one who has raised and drawn three cards, almost certainly to two jokers.

It is advisable in this game to be on guard against being bluffed by the opener. When an opener draws one card to a straight or flush and misses out, he will often try a bluff, knowing that he must lose on a showdown.

6. SUMMING UP

Playing this game against persons who know it well, you wouldn't stand much chance unless you had a good knowledge of all the contents of this chapter. But in a game where Deuces Wild is played only occasionally, the following condensed advice might be sufficient:

1. Open with triplets including a joker or better, or any four-card straight flush, or a four-card straight with a joker and only one gap in the sequence of natural cards.

2. Stay with the above hands and possibly also with natural triplets or a joker and four odd cards if your position is favorable. Raise with two Aces and a joker, or a pat straight or flush, or two jokers.

3. With two jokers, keep an odd Ace if you have one, and draw one card to a straight flush if you can. Otherwise, draw three cards. Don't aim at simple straights or flushes.

4. Stand pat with a straight or flush, even if it contains two jokers, unless it is clear that this can't win the pot.

5. After the draw, a straight is about the minimum hand worth a raise, and often with this hand it is best to check.

CHAPTER EIGHT

OTHER VARIATIONS OF DRAW POKER

Draw Poker, unlike Stud, has not been very prolific of variations. We are now dealing with games that are played only as occasional variations.

1. SPIT IN THE OCEAN

Each player is dealt four cards, and one final card is dealt face up in the center. (Originally this up card was dealt during the deal when one player called out "Spit.") This card, which is common to all hands, is wild, and so are the other three cards of the same denomination.

With every player holding one joker for certain and with three other jokers on the loose, hands are fantastically high. Four of a kind is the average winning hand. A full house will sometimes collect a pot, but flushes and straights are worthless.

Before the Draw

Minimum requirements for opening or staying are as follows (not counting the common joker):

1. Another joker, or
2. A pair of Kings or Aces, or
3. Two pairs. With the joker in the center, this makes a pat full house. This is a possible winner, though by no means a certain one. In fact, if the pot is raised before the draw, it is best to discard the lower pair and draw two cards in the hopes of making four or five of a kind.

To raise before the draw you need triplets in your hand, making four of a kind in all, or a straight flush.

After the Draw

Four of a kind or even a full house are possible winners, but it is scarcely worth while to raise with less than four Aces. A second raise after the draw usually means five of a kind.

2. DRAW POKER WITH WILD CARDS

An infinite number of rather pointless variations can be made by making wild cards of all one-eyed Jacks, say, or all heart honors, or all spades.

The following table of average winning hands will give a clue how to compete.

With	two jokers	Three of a kind
"	five jokers	Flush
"	eight jokers	Four of a kind
"	thirteen jokers	Five of a kind

3. PROGRESSIVE JACKPOTS

A Jackpot is sometimes played under the local rule that if it is not opened, the next hand is a Queen pot. If that is passed out, there is a King pot, then an Ace pot, then down to a King pot, and so on. This goes on until the pot is opened. The ante is usually sweetened each time by one chip from each player.

The game is very similar to an ordinary Jackpot, except that when the requirements are higher than Jacks, the opener must be credited with rather more than in a Jackpot. The opener of a Queen pot, for instance, will hold on average a pair of Aces.

4. JACKS BACK

This is simply a convenient way of introducing Lowball into the cycle of games. A Jackpot is played under the rule that if no one opens, the pot is played for again, without a new deal, as Lowball. This avoids the nuisance of a fresh deal when a Jackpot is not opened, which is quite common in a five- or six-handed game, and obviously when nobody has a good hand, you may well get an interesting game of Lowball.

5. SHOTGUN

The rules here are as for Straight Draw Poker except that a round of betting takes place after the third, fourth and fifth cards have been dealt. With the post-draw betting, this makes a total of four betting intervals.

This game should be played without an ante or else the two extra betting intervals will pyramid the pot up to a size out of all proportion to the usual run of games.

Like all games with several betting intervals, this game must be played tight. To open or stay for the fourth card it is advisable to have a three-card straight or flush or three high cards. At the fourth card you need a pair or a four-card straight or flush. From then on the standards of straight draw apply.

In an extension of this game known as "Double-Barreled Shotgun," after the draw the hands are placed face down on the table and each player "rolls," i.e., he turns up one card, after which there is the fourth betting interval. Each surviving player then rolls another card, and this is followed by the fifth betting interval, and so on, if need be, to the showdown after seven betting intervals. This game is seldom played, interesting though it sounds in theory, for in real life a hand of poker with seven betting intervals is impractical.

6. HIGH-LOW DRAW POKER

In High-Low Poker, the pot is divided between the highest and lowest hands. Pots tend to become large because of the increased number of active players, and sometimes raises before the draw may be restricted to, say, three or four in number. High-Low Draw is played less frequently than High-Low Stud, but it is a good game, and not the shambles that one might expect.

Principles of Play

Before the draw, assume that half the competitors are going for the same half of the pot as yourself, and then value and play your hand as in straight high or low draw. In calculating the odds in chips, remember you can win only half the total pot.

It is usually worth staying for one raise even with minimum requirements, since it is an even money chance that the raise does not concern your half of the pot.

The draw will generally give you some indication of the competition against your own hand. A three-card draw must be going high, unless he is an incurable optimist. A two-card draw in a tight game is probably going high, though in a small-limit game two-card draws may often be made to a low three-card six or seven. A one-card draw is rather more likely to be going low than high, and a pat hand much more likely.

It is, of course, only competition in your own half of the pot that affects the value of your hand. When you are certain it is limited to the other half of the pot, you can raise and go on raising on what in itself may be a poor hand.

Example. "A," "B" and "C" only have stayed for the draw. "A" draws one card to 8 7 3 4, and gets a Jack. "B" and "C" both draw three cards. Here "A's" hand, though not by any means a good low hand, is a certain winner low, since surely "B" and "C" must have at least a pair apiece.

"B," if he has a good hand, is in an awkward position. If he raises, he may be re-raised by "C" and he certainly will be re-raised by "A." He therefore needs a probable overwhelming superiority over his true opponent, "C," for a raise to be worthwhile.

Sometimes it may be worth-while to change the draw you originally intended and switch to where there appears to be less competition.

Example. Only "A," "B" and "C" have stayed for the draw. "A" and "B" draw three cards. "C," holding 10 10 3 6 4, realizes that all the competition is high. He therefore discards one ten and draws one card. Unless he is unlucky enough to get another ten, he is an almost certain winner low, for "A" and "B" must have at least a pair each.

CHAPTER NINE

FIVE CARD STUD

This is the original and basic game of Stud. It can be criticized on the grounds that it favors the tight player and discourages the free bettor. Competition is often strangled before it can develop, particularly in a large-limit game.

Each player is dealt one card face down (the "hole" card) and the rest face up. There is a round of betting after each up card, and the best hand showing always bets first. If there is a showdown, the hole cards of the survivors are turned up and the best hand wins. It sounds a simple game, and so it is in essence, but there is a great deal of play in it nevertheless.

With only five pat cards to each player, a high pair is good enough to win the average pot. But because of the four betting intervals it can cost a surprising amount of money to reach the showdown, and the general aim of play is to win the pot or not get involved in it at all. This isn't a game of percentages, and even in a small-limit game it doesn't pay to trail along on mere hope.

At the Second Card

This is the first interval of betting. You have seen your own hole card, and you can see the up cards of all your opponents.

If the ante is 1 chip or nothing (the usual game) and the opening bet is limited to 1 chip, there isn't much of a problem for anybody. If you are the highest hand showing, and therefore the first to bet, you bet 1 chip. If someone else bets first you can risk 1 chip on almost anything. Even if you have a pair back to back, or an Ace in the hole, don't raise. There is no point in revealing a strong hole card at this stage.

If the ante is, say, 5 chips from the dealer and the game is pot limit, then things are not quite so simple. If you are highest hand showing, you will normally bet 5 chips, the size of the pot. The only possible exception to this is if your up card, though the highest showing, is a low card and your hole card is also a low card. You have a weak hand and might reasonably open for 1 chip or even pass. Some players also open for 1 chip with a King as up card and another King in the hole. This may attract some players in who might otherwise have folded, but the sandbag is a bit too obvious to have much advantage.

If another player makes an opening bet of 5 chips you should stay only if you have:

1. A Jack or better in the hole. Or
2. A higher hole card than any up card showing. Or
3. A pair.

These may sound like very tight requirements, but there are three more betting intervals and you can save a lot of money by not becoming involved with an unpromising hand.

As we have already said, there is no point in raising at this stage even with a pair or an Ace in the hole.

At the Third Card

This is the second interval of betting. If you are the best hand showing, bet the limit up to the size of the pot. You don't want everyone trailing along cheaply, and your bet is really to protect your hand.

If another player bets first, fold if your three cards cannot beat his two up cards. Even if you have a pair it would be wrong to stay if there is a higher open pair against you, unless the limit is small and the pot crowded so that you are getting long odds in chips. There is an old Stud maxim which says, "If you can't raise at the third card, fold." This is perhaps going too far, but it is a mistake in the right direction. Certainly in any large-limit game, unless you positively think you are going to win you shouldn't go on to the fourth card.

A raise is in order when all of the following conditions exist:

1. You have paired your hole card, which is something between a nine and a King. (A pair of eights is not good enough for a raise, and a pair of Aces is too good.)

2. There are no other pairs showing, and the betting has not indicated that anyone has a pair.

3. There are several competitors for the pot.

The reason for the raise is mainly protective. Your hand is probably the best so far. But if you allow everyone to trail along cheaply, you may not end up on top.

With a pair of Aces it is usually best not to start putting on pressure at this stage. An Ace in the hole loses much of its value if you disclose it too early.

At the Fourth Card

This is the turning point of the pot, when the betting really starts to get lethal. The highest hand showing, provided no one else has been raising aggressively, should again bet the size of the pot. To bet less indicates either that you have a very weak hole card or that you have paired your high up card and are trying to coax everyone into stringing along.

If another player is first to bet, again the general rule is to fold unless with your four cards you can beat his three up cards. However, there are occasions when you can relax this rule: If, for instance, there are no pairs showing and your second and third cards look as though they may win if you can pair them.

Example. "A" has ?6 4 J. You have 8 10 3 9. (Note that the hole cards are underlined, the cards were dealt in the order given, and, unless otherwise stated, the cards are in different suits. These rules will be followed in all example hands.) In this case, it is worth staying because if you pair your eight, nine or ten at the fifth card, you stand a chance of winning the pot.

Against an open pair, the best course normally is to fold. Here is where "carding" comes in handy. Carding means watching the cards carefully as they are exposed, and remembering the cards of players who have retired. This is obviously an important weapon in the poker player's arsenal, for carding may sometimes suggest a more optimistic policy in the betting than the rules might dictate.

Example. "A" has ? 8 6 6 and bets the size of the pot. You have K Q 10 7. The other five players retired after the second up card, and their cards were ? 8 2, ? 9 2, ? J 8, ? 5 6, ? 6 4. In this case, the cards are very favorable to you. There are no outstanding sixes and only one outstanding eight to help "A," whereas no Kings, Queens, tens or sevens have yet appeared. Of the 35 outstanding cards, 12 will give you a pair, or 1 in 3. Although there is, of course, no guarantee that "A" has not, or will not have, two pairs, at least your chances are bright enough to go on for the fifth card.

If you feel you could not perform the difficult feat of carding in the give-and-take of an actual poker game with, perhaps, someone offering you a drink and someone else wanting you to change some chips, don't worry. Nor could the others.

At the fourth card you can, for the first time, legitimately consider the possibilities of straights and flushes. Up to now, this factor should have been ignored. It would be quite wrong to stay for a fourth card just because your first three cards happened to be spades. Only the high card values should have been considered, and if these weren't good enough the hand should have been thrown. But if you stayed for other reasons and if the fourth card happens also to be a spade, then the picture changes.

The odds against the fifth card's also being a spade will not be the invariable 4 to 1 as in Draw Poker. By this time you will have seen so many exposed cards that you should be able to make an amended calculation. Suppose you have seen, apart from your own 4 cards, 18 up cards, and of these 2 were spades. This means that 7 of the outstanding 30 cards will be spades. The odds against your final card's being a spade will be, therefore, 3 to 1.

You can, however, accept less than the actual odds in chips, for if you do fill you can always make a substantial bet after the last card. And in this game, flushes and straights are so scarce that bets of this kind are generally called. Apart from this factor, four-card flushes or straights generally contain other possibilities, even if the flush or straight is busted by the last card.

Example. "A" has ? 7 6 7. "B" has ? J 10 10. You have Q 9 10 J in different suits. The betting so far has been unrevealing and you have no reason to suspect that either "A" or "B" has anything terrific in the hole. Even though carding warns you that chances are unfavorable for a straight, your hand has a reasonable chance of winning as a pair of Queens or Jacks.

Raising the first to bet at the fourth card is a dangerous business, and you want to be sure of your grounds. If he has a useful hole card, he will raise you back, for he knows he's got the better hand. But by this time you should have some clue as to his hole card, and this may confirm that you have the best hand at the moment. In this case a raise is in order.

Example. "A" has ? 10 9 Q. You have J 6 J 10. After the second card, i.e., at the first interval of betting, "A" was high and he bet the size of the pot. Several players stayed. After the third card you were high with your exposed Jack. You bet the size of the pot and "A" raised. Everyone dropped out except you.

This raise by "A" surely fixes him with a nine or a ten in the hole. If his hand was Q 10 9 he would never have raised your ? 6 J, so he can't have a Queen in the hole. Your pair of Jacks is worth another raise at the fourth card, being undoubtedly the best hand at the moment.

At the Fifth Card

If you are the highest exposed hand, the best thing to do generally is to check, no matter what your hole card is. If it is worthless, anyone who calls will beat you, for obviously he won't call unless he can beat what you show. If your hole card improves you so that you have an unbeatable hand, your best chance of making money generally is to hope that an opponent will also have concealed strength and will raise. You can then re-raise.

There are exceptions to this rule. If you think that an opponent may be tempted to call a bet, but that there is no chance of his raising if you check, then a bet is in order.

Example. "A" has ? 7 9 10 K. You have A A 4 3 2. You have consistently bet the size of the pot, and "A," who is a sound player, has just as consistently called. What should you do after the fifth card?

In this case you should not check. It is almost certain that "A" has a pair of sevens or nines, or else he would never have stayed against your exposed Ace. If you bet, he may possibly call in the hope that you are bluffing, but if you check he would never raise against that obvious danger of a second Ace in the hole.

The situation at the last card is always dominated by the possibility that the first to bet may be betting on an absolute certainty. For instance, if he has the highest pair showing and a third to it in the hole, he cannot possibly be beaten. Similarly, if there are no pairs showing, and he shows the highest card and has its pair in the hole, he has a certain winner. With a "cinch" or an "immortal," as these hands are called, even the most timid player can bet all he's got, and the danger for his opponents at Table Stakes or in a large-limit game is immense.

It is, therefore, normally unsound to raise the first to bet at the last card, even if you can beat what he shows, and even if he has only checked. If he has a cinch he will re-raise the limit. If his hole card is worthless he will fold. So a raise here is one of those bets, so much to be avoided, that cannot gain you anything and may lose you a lot.

Example. "A" has ? J 10 9 K. You have 9 Q 9 7 3. "A" checks. A raise here by you would be absurd. If "A" hasn't a pair he certainly won't call. And if he has a King or Queen in the hole he has a cinch and will re-raise you.

If your hand was Q 9 Q 7 3, then a raise might have some point, for there is a possibility that "A" might have a Jack or a ten in the hole, and in that case he might well call. A raise in this case may gain you something. A raise against a possible cinch in these circumstances is often justified, particularly if that player never bluffs, so that if he re-raises you need not trouble to see him.

It also sometimes happens that though an opponent has a possible cinch, it is in fact rather unlikely, and at the same time there is a reasonable chance that he will call your bet.

Example. "A" has ? 3 4 10 10. You have 8 A 8 6 8. After each of the first three up cards you bet the size of the pot, and each time "A" called. "A" now checks.

Here you should raise. It is extraordinarily unlikely that "A's" hole card is a ten. He would hardly have stayed against your exposed Ace unless it was a three or a four, and with two pairs he will probably think himself strong enough to call your bet.

Carding may also remove the dangers from a possible cinch.

Example. "A" has ? 9 Q 9 5. "B" has ? K 4 J 9. "C" has ? A 9 5 2. You have 6 6 K 10 6. In this case "A" cannot have a nine in the hole, for all nines are out. This promotes your own hand to immortality.

Summing Up

The foregoing pages can be summed up simply in the following rules of play, which like all rules of play in poker should be followed in principle rather than blindly and invariably.

1. If you are the highest hand showing in the early stages, bet the limit up to the size of the pot.

2. Don't stay in the early stages against any real bet unless you can beat anything showing.

3. If you are first to act at the last card, check.

4. Don't raise a possible cinch.

We might add that if everyone followed these rules religiously Five Card Stud would indeed be a dull game!

GENERAL TACTICS

In this game there is only one unknown factor and that is the identity of the hole cards, but during the course of play numerous clues will be given.

A player who stays against a real bet for a fourth card with two low up-cards obviously has an Ace or a King in the hole, or else he has already paired one of his up cards.

A player who, although highest showing, consistently bet small in the early rounds probably has a pair back to back.

A tipoff which is elementary but amazingly common is that of the player who looks again at his hole card after having been dealt two or three up cards. This invariably means that it is something less than a Jack, for no one is likely to forget a high card in the hole. There is a distinct probability that the card is the same as his last up card, and he is just checking to make absolutely sure. The moral of this is, "Look once and for all time at your hole card, and don't forget it."

A common indication of a valuable hole card is when a player shows more than a natural care to ensure that it isn't turned up by accident, sometimes even to the extent of putting a pile of chips on top of it. Even in the most tumultuous poker game, with the table littered with chips, cards, ash trays and drinks, and maybe a breeze coming through an open window, this is a fatal mistake. You might as well turn it up yourself, and have done with it.

In many pots there is little real competition, and opportunities for bluff are good. The holder of a possible "cinch" is always in a good tactical position if he has checked at the last card and someone has raised. But at all times he must make sure that he has not already revealed his hole card by his past play.

Example. "A" has ? 5 6 7 8. You have 8 K 10 9 K. You have always bet the size of the pot and "A" has always called. At the last card you check, and "A" raises by the size of the pot, suggesting a straight. Should you call? The answer is, yes. "A" would not have stayed in the early rounds if his hole card was a four or a nine. Almost certainly it's an Ace or another five or six. His bluff is a bad one.

If you rigidly follow the rules of play we have given in the foregoing pages you will never play with a low card in the hole unless it matches one of your early up cards. If opponents knew this for certain, it would be a great help to them, for they would always have some clue as to your hole card. Therefore you must sometimes break the rules, just to "advertise." You must vary your play on this and other points, and this is even more important in Stud than in Draw, for in Stud you have so little to conceal. Just the one hole card!

For instance, if you have immense concealed strength, say Aces back to back, the correct technical play is to bet lightly in the early betting intervals and so avoid driving out all your competitors. But against a shrewd opponent this may be too obvious. He may correctly interpret your small bets. This type of player is actually more likely to stay against a big bet, which he will interpret as an effort to protect your hand.

SMALL LIMIT STUD

We have throughout suggested tactics which are distinctly tight, on the assumption that the limit is large. In this sort of game tight play is essential. But Stud, of course, can be played with a small limit. A good system is no ante, a one-chip limit for the first betting interval, a five-chip limit for the next two intervals, and a ten-chip limit for the final betting interval, if an open pair appears on the table.

With this limit you can relax the standards we have suggested, particularly in the last stages when you may be getting good odds in chips. Bet boldly whenever you have the best hand, and forget all about the dangers of betting into a possible cinch. He can only raise you back 10 chips, and that's not a very serious matter.

PROBLEMS AND ANSWERS

Problem 1. "A" has ? 6 K. You, sitting at "B," have 10 Q 10. "C" has ? 9 J. "D" has ? 10 Q. "A" bets the size of the pot. What should you do?

Answer. You should raise. Your hand is probably the best so far. But if you allow everyone to trail along with their high card values, your pair of tens are not likely to stand up. It will pay you to try to keep down the numbers.

Problem 2. The betting has been noncommittal and the position after the fifth card is as follows: "A," your only remaining opponent, has ? 10 8 Q 3. You have K 8 9 J J. What should you do?

Answer. You should check. If you bet, and "A" hasn't got a Queen in the hole, he won't call. So your bet can't win you money whereas it might lose you some.

Problem 3. "A," your only opponent, has ? 6 K 3 2. You have 8 8 Q J 7. "A" checks. What should you do? (The game is Table Stakes.)

Answer. You should check also. You may well win at the showdown, but the point is that "A" may have a King in the hole, in which case he has a cinch and will tap. In principle, one should avoid betting into possible immortals, at least in a large-limit game.

CHAPTER TEN

SEVEN CARD STUD

Sometimes called "Down the River," this is a somewhat freer version of Five Card Stud and is a regular feature of almost every poker game. Pots tend to be larger than in straight Stud, as described in the previous chapter, as there is one more betting interval and betting in general is apt to be more liberal.

Two cards are dealt face down and four cards face up, an interval of betting taking place after each up card. The highest hand showing, as in all Stud games, is first to act, and checking is usually allowed in all but the first betting interval. The seventh and last card is dealt face down, or down the river, and is followed by the fifth and final betting interval. At the showdown any five cards of the seven can be used to make up the best poker hand.

The technique of playing this game is completely different from Five Card Stud. There is much less information to be obtained from the up cards of opponents, who may at the finish hold four of a kind without even a pair showing. The game has, in fact, rather more in common with Draw Poker, for the values of the hands are about the same. Two pairs or three of a kind is the average winning hand. With three cards concealed, cinches occur so rarely they aren't worth mentioning.

At the Early Cards

Betting is usually fairly mild during the early betting intervals. The two hole cards present such unknown dangers that the first to bet, although highest showing, has no reason to suppose he is the highest hand, and will usually check or bet one chip. Any real bet at an early stage can be taken to indicate a very promising hand.

At the third card you should have either a pair or a three-card straight or flush or two high cards. With any of these, open for the size of the pot if there is an ante, or, stay against a pot-sized opening bet. If you have less than this, but happen to be highest showing, bet one chip. (If there is no ante you can only bet one chip whatever your hand, of course.)

At the fourth card, and second interval of betting, you should fold without a medium pair or a four-card straight or flush or a three-card straight flush. Lessen these requirements if you can string along for one or two chips.

It may sound excessively tight not to stay for a fifth card with a three-card straight or flush in your first four cards, but the mathematics of the situation are against it. The odds against ending up with a straight or flush are 8 to 1. Although you can accept less than this, say 6 to 1 (for if you do fill you are surely going to win quite a lot of extra chips in the end betting), even 6 to 1 will not often be obtainable. Of course a player who always stays in these circumstances will eventually get his straight or flush, but it is certain that his gains will not cover all the chips lost in the process.

With either threes or a four-card straight or flush at the fourth card, you have an excellent hand and can consider a raise, though very often you will make more money in the long run by sitting back at this stage. With two pairs at this stage you should always raise, provided you have no reason to fear concealed strength somewhere. The object of this raise is protective. You have quite a good hand, but it is unlikely to improve. If you can keep down competition you stand a better chance of collecting the pot without having improved.

After the fifth card you should fold without at least a pair of Jacks or a four-card straight or flush. And if a third card to your pair has been shown elsewhere, the hand is worth no more than a chip or two. Two pairs if lower than Queens up have only a doubtful raising value at this stage. Anything better is certainly worth a raise.

At the Sixth and Seventh Cards

By this time you should have some idea of the opposition, not so much from the exposed cards as from the betting. Also by now there will have been a considerable number of cards exposed, perhaps nearly half the pack. This will considerably affect the chances of the various hands. For instance, a potential flush in diamonds opposite becomes much less dangerous if a large number of diamonds have been shown in other hands. Your pair of Kings becomes much less valuable if another King has shown up somewhere else, and still less so if a fourth King turns up in another hand.

If no serious betting is taking place, a high pair is worth playing provided that no card of that denomination has appeared elsewhere. If it has, your chances of making three of a kind are so reduced that they aren't worth taking. True, you still have a fair chance of ending up with two pairs, but two pairs is no more than a possible winner. And in any form of poker it is a good idea to make sure that the hand you are aiming to make is good enough to be at least a very probable winner.

Two pairs, as in Draw Poker, is the really tricky hand to play. It is unlikely to improve by the seventh card, yet as it stands it has a fair chance of winning the average pot. If you can reach the showdown cheaply, by all means do so. But a raise is out of the question, and if an opponent who shows a higher pair makes a real bet, even a call is a doubtful proposition. It all depends on whether you think he's bluffing or not.

A four-card straight or flush is nearly always worth staying for a sixth card and generally for a seventh, particularly if you have more than one opponent. There are two exceptions. One is when so many of your wanted cards have been exposed elsewhere that your chances of filling have become negligible. For instance, suppose you have a four-card diamond flush, there has been a total of 16 up cards including your own, and 4 diamonds have been shown by opponents. Of the 34 outstanding cards, 5 are diamonds, which means it is nearly 6 to 1 against your drawing a diamond. At these odds, staying for a pot-sized bet would be futile.

The other exception is when it appears that even if you do fill you may not win the pot.

Example. You have 5 8 7 6 K 2, in different suits. An opponent has ? ? K J 10 9, also in different suits. He bets the size of the pot. There is here a possibility (*a*) that you won't fill, and (*b*) that even if you do fill, your opponent may have a higher straight. A seventh card is definitely not worth the price.

End betting after the seventh card is not complicated by the possibility of cinches. If you are first to bet, and think you have the best hand, bet heavily, unless you think a trap pass will gain you more. And go on raising so long as you think you have the best hand. But never forget that an opponent may show nothing and yet have four of a kind.

The above rules of play apply to a large-limit game. In a small-limit game, if you have survived to the fifth card, you will be getting such good odds in chips that it is usually worth-while continuing on to the showdown on any reasonable chance.

PROBLEMS AND ANSWERS

Problem 1. "A" has ? ? Q 7. "B" has ? ? J 8. You have 3 4 3 5, in various suits. There are 5 chips in the pot, and "A" bets 5 chips. "B" stays. What should you do?

Answer. You should stay. The pair of threes would not alone justify staying, nor would the three-card straight in the first four cards. But together they make it worth-while. Besides, the fact that one card of the pair is concealed gives the hand a slight extra value.

Problem 2. "A," who bet heavily at the sixth card, has ? ? A 3 3 A ?. You have 10 Q 10 J 2 9 K, in various suits. "A" checks. What should you do?

Answer. If the limit is large you should check also. "A" must suspect you of holding a straight, and if you bet and he hasn't a full house he probably won't call. If he has he will raise. In a small-limit game a raise would be justified, for you can't come to much harm even if he does raise you back.

CHAPTER ELEVEN

OTHER STUD VARIATIONS

There are an almost unlimited number of Stud Poker variations. To add to the confusion they often masquerade under different names, and there are also variations of variations. We do not pretend that this chapter is exhaustive or that the games we mention are invariably played exactly as described.

For the most part, the games in this chapter do not feature in serious large-limit poker, but small-limit poker can become dull without a fair amount of variety. Contrary to popular belief, the greater the number of variations played, the higher the skill factor, particularly in the technical sense.

1. BASEBALL

This is a really excellent game which even the most conservative poker player could hardly fail to enjoy. The game is Seven Card Stud (Down the River) with the following additions:

1. All nines are wild.

2. A player who receives an exposed trey (three) must either fold or pay into the pot an agreed penalty. If he elects to pay the penalty, all treys become wild. (The penalty is generally 10 chips but is sometimes the size of the pot. It should be a fairly substantial amount, large enough to act as a possible deterrent. The whole point of the game is the uncertainty as to whether there are going to be four wild cards or eight.)

3. A player who receives an exposed four has the option of discarding it immediately and getting another card in its place.

The difficulty in this game is that at the showdown there may be four jokers, in which case a flush will probably be good enough to collect the pot, or there may be eight jokers, in which case high four of a kind is the average winning hand, and straight flushes and fives by no means uncommon.

At the outset it is best to act on the assumption that there will be eight jokers. Minimum requirements for staying for the fourth card are a nine or a three among your first three cards, or a natural pair, or a three-card straight flush. By the fifth card you should have at least a natural pair plus your nine or threes, or a four-card straight flush.

With two nines and no treys in the hole, you can consider a raise with the object of driving out some of the competition and reducing the chances of treys becoming wild. If only nines are wild at the showdown your hand should be a near certain winner.

If no treys have been turned up by the fifth card, and especially if a trey has been dealt but the recipient did not choose to stay for the penalty, you must begin to consider your hand in the light of a four-joker showdown. Your trey in the hole becomes just a trey and not a potential joker.

Example. "A" has <u>?</u> <u>?</u> K 4 9. "B" has <u>?</u> <u>?</u> J 8 J, "C" has <u>?</u> <u>?</u> 10 8 3. You have <u>3</u> <u>10</u> 7 Q 10. "C" declines to pay the penalty. "A" bets the limit. "B" calls. What should you do?

"A" clearly has at least three fours, for he would only have stuck to his four if he had another four in the hole. "B" probably has at least three Jacks. Your pair of tens is a hopeless proposition. If treys don't become jokers the most you can reasonably hope for is three tens, a useless hand. And even if you are lucky enough to get an up trey on the sixth card, all you'll most likely have at the showdown is four tens, a pretty indifferent hand in an eight-joker showdown. You should fold.

If you yourself are dealt an exposed trey, do not stay for the penalty automatically (unless of course the penalty is trivial compared to the size of the pot). Only pay if your hand looks like a good odds-on bet for winning the pot. If your trey is your last up card you should have at least four of a kind or a four-card straight flush.

If this game is played with the penalty so small that anyone who gets a trey will pay it automatically, it loses much of its interest. It is a virtual certainty that a trey will turn up somewhere and the game becomes merely Seven Card Stud with eight jokers. Average winning hand is high fours, and nothing less than a straight flush or fives is really worth getting excited about. The general principle of play is not to stay unless you have a reasonably good chance of ending up with something better than four of a kind.

2. CINCINNATI

This game is a mixture of Stud and Draw. Five cards are dealt to each player as in Draw, and five extra cards are dealt face down in the center. These center cards are known as the "widow." The center cards are turned up one at a time, and a round of betting takes place after each card. Each player makes the best poker hand out of his own and the center cards. There are, therefore, five intervals of betting and each player who stays to the end will have ten cards, five concealed cards of his own and five common up cards in the widow.

This is a good game with lots of possibilities. Average winning hand is something between a flush and a full house.

Straights should be ignored and, for the most part, flushes also, on the sound old poker maxim for Stud that if the hand you are aiming at isn't a near-certain winner if you get it, then you should fold. However, flushes are worth a try if all the following conditions are fulfilled:

1. You can stay fairly cheaply.

2. You are fairly certain to get your flush. This means having three or four of the suit in your own hand, and four anyway by the seventh card.

3. There is no pair on the table. If there is, there is nearly certain to be a full house somewhere.

If there are three cards of another suit on the table, it is very likely that someone has a flush in that suit. In this case the high cards of the two flushes must be considered.

With no potential flush, stay only with a very high pair in the hand, which improves to two pairs or threes in the first one or two up cards.

After this it is a matter of making deductions from the betting and the up cards. If you finally finish up with a full house and there is no pair on the table, you have an excellent hand. If there is a pair on the table and the threes of your full house are higher than the pair on the table, then you still have a very good hand. But watch out if your threes are lower than the pair in the widow. There is a distinct risk of another and better full house against you.

3. SEVEN CARD STUD WITH THE BUG

This is quite a good game. The Bug, it will be remembered, is a joker which can be used as an Ace or as part of a straight or flush.

On the third card, or first interval of betting, only stay with a three-card straight or flush or a high pair or the Bug. And if the Bug shows up against you, you must have a fair chance for a flush or full house to make staying worth-while. Raising on a four-card straight which includes the Bug is sound at the fourth or fifth card.

The Bug obviously makes flushes more common and straights comparatively frequent, but it should not completely dominate the game.

4. LOW FIVE CARD STUD

This is quite a good game, different from other forms of Stud in that no one can have concealed strength. A player can only conceal his weakness. For instance, an opponent shows $\underline{?}$ 6 4 J. His hand cannot be better than Jack high, though it might be worse.

The average winning hand in this game is Jack high. With nothing higher than a Jack, or if you can beat everything in sight, stay for a third or fourth card.

At the fourth card, if you can beat everything showing, bet out boldly. Do not be put off by a large number of competitors. You have a good odds-on chance of winning the pot, and the more chips you can get into it, the better.

If you are beaten in sight at the fourth card (it must be assumed that anyone who is betting has neither a pair nor a high hole card), stay if you are lying second. You have approximately 1 chance in 3 of ending up on top. If beaten by two competitors the odds against you are 6 to 1, and this means that it is scarcely ever worth staying.

The situation at the last card is similar to that of straight Five Card Stud. The best hand showing may be an immortal and, more often than not, will be. If you have reason to think he is bluffing, that his last card paired his hole card, call him. Obviously, you will not re-raise.

If you yourself have the best hand showing but have been wrecked by your hole card, the only way you can possibly win the pot is to bluff. You should always give serious consideration to this though of course it's not worth doing against a player who cannot be bluffed.

Example. You have 6 10 4 2 6. An opponent shows ? 9 3 7 Q. It is almost certain that your opponent has no pair. He would not have stayed for the fifth card if his hole card was a nine, a three, a seven or a Queen. So if you check, you must lose. Your only chance of winning is to bluff, leaving your opponent with an awkward decision.

5. MEXICAN STUD or FLIP

In this variation of Five Card Stud, each player gets two down cards to start with, and he can turn up, or "roll," whichever one he chooses. The next card is also dealt face down and each player has the choice of rolling it or keeping it face down and rolling his original hole card. He has the same choice at the fourth and fifth cards which are likewise originally dealt face down. At each interval of betting, therefore, each player has one hole card of his own choice.

In this game the old Stud rule—betting the size of the pot as a matter of principle if you are the highest hand showing—must go overboard. Obviously each player will normally start by concealing his highest card, so in the early rounds it is your hole card that dictates your policy. If the chances are that it's beaten elsewhere, there's not much point in stringing along.

If an opponent rolls an Ace, that normally means he has a pair. And if he rolls one of a pair, that indicates on the face of it two pairs or threes. But of course rolling cards may be used as an element of bluff. A player may show a low pair with nothing in the hole, and bet high in the hopes of driving everyone out.

This is a very good game with plenty of scope for psychological strategy.

6. FIVE CARD STUD WITH THE BUG

Five Card Stud can be played with the Bug, but it doesn't make a very good game.

Potential straights and flushes become more valuable unless the Bug has turned up in another hand. Otherwise, their chances of improving are greatly increased.

The chief objection to the game is that it tends to become rather Ace-conscious. The appearance of an Ace or the Bug as an up card is often the signal for everyone else to pack up, and quite rightly.

7. NEW YORK STUD

In this variant of Five Card Stud a four flush beats a pair but loses to two pairs or better. This opens up the game quite a bit.

8. SHIFTING SANDS

This is a variation of Mexican Stud. The first two cards are dealt face down, and each player can choose his own hole card and turn up the other. His hole card and the three others of the same denomination are wild so far as his own hand is concerned. The next three cards are also dealt face down, the player having the choice of turning each one up or keeping it face down as his new hole card instead of his former hole card. Each player will therefore always have one hole card, but it may not always be the same card.

9. WOOLWORTH

Seven Card Stud with all fives and tens wild. An up five attracts a penalty of 5 chips if the holder wishes to stay, and an up ten, 10 chips.

Four of a kind has a good chance of winning a pot, but you need a straight flush or five of a kind really to bet out.

10. FOOTBALL

Seven Card Stud with sixes and fours wild. An up four attracts a penalty of the size of the pot if the holder wishes to stay. An up deuce entitles the holder to an extra hole card.

Rather similar to Woolworth, but don't pay that heavy penalty unless you have a good chance of ending with something better than five of a kind.

11. DOCTOR PEPPER

Seven Card Stud with all deuces, fours and tens wild.

Nothing much less than a straight flush is worth pursuing in this game.

12. LOW HOLE CARD WILD

This is Seven Card Stud with your lowest hole card wild, as well as the other three cards of the same denomination.

The point of the game is that unless one of your first two hole cards is a deuce, you cannot be sure that the last card will not ruin your hand, though of course you must end with at least one joker. By the fifth card you should have high three of a kind or a four-card straight flush.

13. KANKAKEE

This is the Seven Card Stud version of Spit in the Ocean. The first card is dealt into the middle face up, is wild and is presumed to belong to all hands. After that the game proceeds as in Seven Card Stud except that only six cards are given to each player, the first two down, the next three up, and the final card down. Four of a kind is the average winning hand.

14. BEDSPRINGS

This is a variation of Cincinnati. Each player is dealt five cards as in Draw. Then ten cards are dealt face down in the center in two rows of five cards each. The center cards are turned up one at a time, the top row first, an interval of betting taking place after each card. At the showdown a player may use any five cards from his own hand or from one of the "bedsprings" in the center. A bedspring is the two corresponding cards, one in the top row, one in the bottom. For instance, the first card in the top row and the first card in the other row form a bedspring.

15. CINCINNATI LIZ

The rules are as for Cincinnati except that the lowest exposed card and the other three cards of the same denomination are wild.

CHAPTER TWELVE

HIGH-LOW STUD

This is a very sophisticated form of poker which requires great concentration. It is mostly played with a small limit, say 5 chips increasing to 10 at the last betting interval or when an open pair shows on the table. The number of raises in any interval except the last is restricted to three. If played pot limit and without restrictions on the number of raises, the game can get astronomically high. The pot is divided between the highest and lowest hands.

1. HIGH-LOW FIVE CARD STUD

This game is not played very often although it is quite an interesting one.

When aiming high, play more or less as in straight Stud, making due allowance for those who appear to be going for the other half of the pot. They are not always easy to spot. A string of low cards may be accompanied by an Ace in the hole or the hole card may pair an up card. Nor are opponents who are genuinely going low to be entirely discounted when you are aiming high. A perfect three-card low can be turned into a formidable high hand by the last two cards.

When aiming low, play rather more freely than in straight Low Stud, since there is always the possibility that a dangerous-looking low hand opposite may in fact be aiming high.

Cinches, both high and low, are fairly common. The rule of not raising a possible cinch still holds good in a large-limit game, though of course it only applies to cinches in your own half. Sometimes even calling a possible cinch is dangerous since if there is a cinch in the other half he will re-raise.

This game is sometimes played with the option of turning up the hole card and taking the last card face down. A player with four good low cards will normally do this, for it gives him a chance of winning by a bluff if his last card ruins his hand. Consequently, a player with three low cards showing who takes his last card face up may be presumed to have a high hole card or a pair. Naturally a good player must vary his play from time to time so that no such certain deductions can be made.

2. HIGH-LOW SEVEN CARD STUD

This is the great high-low game. Most people who play it regularly agree that it is the best of all poker games. It is significant that this is the only poker game that addicts are happy to play continuously and exclusively.

The secret is to play much more tightly than in ordinary Seven Card Stud when aiming high, and rather freely when aiming low. The reason for this is that many hands that are developing well for low are also potential straights or, less frequently, potential flushes. This gives them a two-way chance, with the additional possibility of winning both ways and collecting the entire pot. With seven cards to choose from at the showdown, each player has in effect two hands and may therefore win both high and low. For instance, 2 3 4 5 6 A is both a straight and a six low. The betting does not therefore necessarily stop when the competitors are reduced to two.

The player aiming high, and with no low prospects, is at a disadvantage and should be careful not to get involved in a big pot unless he has a reasonable chance of getting a straight or better. This particularly applies to a large-limit game.

Ignore this, and you may find yourself in the despairing position of having only one opponent who has already won low (low cinches are common since everyone must use at least two of his up cards in his final hand) and has a chance of winning high as well. He will obviously bet the limit wherever possible, for he has everything to gain and nothing to lose by so doing. He must get back his own stake, for he gets half the pot whatever happens. And he may win the entire pot. Conversely any further bets by you are pointless. The best you can hope for is to get them back.

Example. "A" has Q 7 Q Q 9 J. "B," his only opponent, has ? ? 10 8 6 7. There are 100 chips in the pot, and "B" now bets a further 100 chips. (The limit is Pot Limit.)

To reach the showdown "A" will have to stake 100 chips now, and a further 300 which "B" will certainly bet after the last card. If "B" does not get his straight, "A" will get back his 400 chips plus 50 which represents his net profit on the transaction. If "B" does get his straight, and if "A" does not improve to a full house or fours, "A" loses 400 chips. He is, in fact, risking 400 chips to win 50, an 8 to 1 on bet. It can't be worth it, and "A" should fold his three Queens, however nice they look, before the seventh card.

The exception is a small-limit game, or in Table Stakes where either "A" or "B" has only a few chips. Then "A" can reach the showdown cheaply and should stay.

Another type of cinch that is fairly common when the competitors are reduced to two is a hand that must win either high or low. Here again the holder should always raise the limit. He must get his stake back, and he may scare his opponent away and collect the entire pot.

Example. "A" has Q 2 4 6 7 Q 10. "B" has ? ? 2 3 J J ? . If "B" has a Jack or a deuce or a trey or another pair in the hole, "A" must win low since "B's" low hand cannot be better than Jack low. If "B" has three good low cards in the hole, then "A" must win high. "A" should, therefore, bet the limit, and if "B's" hand is something like 8 4 2 3 J J 9, he may not be willing to take the risk of calling and being beaten both ways.

This game is often played under Contract rules. When the betting in the last interval is completed, and before the showdown, the surviving players must declare in turn whether they are aiming high or low or both ways. A player can only win according to this declaration. If he declares both ways, he must win both high and low to win anything. The first player to make his declaration is the last player who raised. If everyone checked at the last betting interval, the best hand showing on the table makes the first declaration. After that the survivors declare in rotation to the left.

The last to declare obviously has a big tactical advantage in that he can aim where the competition appears least. The first to declare is in the worst possible position. In that situation, unless you are very sure of your grounds, don't be too keen on raising in the last betting interval.

3. HIGH-LOW CINCINNATI

The technique for playing high is the same as in Straight Cincinnati, as described in the previous chapter. Though the competition against your own hand is less clear-cut, the winning hand will still generally be a flush or a full house.

The winning low hand is generally very near the perfect low. Stay only with four near-perfect cards in the hand, or three perfect ones. The latter is really a borderline case, since a low hand which includes two up cards is always a doubtful holding. Even if it is a perfect low there is a good chance that an opponent will have an exactly similar hand, and if there is only one player going high you may find yourself taking less out of the pot than you put into it. (Because of the danger of ties low, it is better to be aiming high rather than low at this game.)

Many hands start with possibilities both ways. Take 10 10 7 3 2, for instance. This hand would be worth following up for one or two cards anyway, though the individual high and low possibilities are fairly poor. A pair of tens is certainly not worth staying for high on its own merits alone, and 7 3 2 for low is also worthless.

As the pot progresses it is important to take warning from up cards which do not happen to help you but which may easily help someone going the same way as yourself.

Example. You have in your hand 9 7 6 4 3. The first up card in the widow is a King, the second a Jack and the third a trey. The trey has done you no good, but almost certainly it has helped some other low hand. Your hand is not now very promising and should be thrown in.

CHAPTER THIRTEEN

ENGLISH STUD

This is the standard Stud game in England, Australia and South Africa. In most London gambling clubs it is the only form of Stud allowed. In America the game is virtually unknown. (Where played in America, it is sometimes called "poker with options.") This is a pity, as it is a fascinating and exciting game which combines the best features of Draw Poker, straight Stud and Seven Card Stud. It is a highly skilled game, perhaps the most difficult of all poker games to play well.

It is played as follows:

The first two cards are dealt face down, the third card face up. Everyone looks at his own hole cards, and the first betting interval takes place.

When the bets have been completed, the fourth card is given face up to the survivors, followed by the second interval of betting. Then a fifth card, followed by the third interval of betting. (So far, the game is exactly like Seven Card Stud.)

Now the first discard takes place. Starting from the left of the dealer—and it is important to discard strictly in order—players either discard an up card or a down card as they wish. If a player discards an up card, he receives the sixth card face up. If he discards a down card, he receives the sixth card face down. A player may also stand pat. When the discarding and replacement is completed, the fourth betting interval takes place.

Notice that from the fifth card onwards each surviving player always has two down and three up cards.

1. GENERAL TACTICS

The level of final hands is slightly less than in Seven Card Stud, because the discarding makes it rather more difficult to improve a pair in the first five cards. However, the same standards for staying and raising in the early betting intervals apply more or less. In the discarding phase the game becomes rather like Draw Poker, and you have to watch percentages. In the end betting the game becomes rather like straight Stud in that you have to watch out for possible cinches.

Assuming a large-limit game, this is how to play at various stages:

1. *First betting interval*, after three cards. If you have the highest up card, you may as well open for the limit. In practice, it will probably be, only 1 chip, since this game is played, or should be played, without an ante. If someone else opens, stay if you have an Ace or King in the hole, or if you have two high cards, or a two-card straight or flush. Raise if you have a pair or a three-card straight or flush.

2. *Second betting interval*, after four cards. A three-card straight is a doubtful proposition at this stage. If you are first to bet, check or bet one chip. If someone else bets first, fold if he makes a real bet. The same rules apply if your hand is no better than four high cards, with no straight or flush potential. Raise with a pair, unless there is an open pair against you. This raise is protective. You don't want too many opponents. In particular, you don't want to give a cheap ride to those with vague hopes of a straight or flush. Raise also with two pairs, or a four-card open straight or flush.

3. *Third betting interval*, after five cards. By this time, much depends on how the others are betting and what sort of hands are showing. A low pair is a doubtful proposition if anyone is betting seriously. Stay normally with a high pair, and even raise if it looks as if you have the best hand so far. In assessing the value of a pair at this or any other time, you must take note of whether

there is or has been another card of that denomination showing. If there is, that cuts in half your chances of making triplets. Raise with two pairs: you won't win unless you can keep down the number of competitors. Raise also with a four-card straight or flush.

With a four-card straight or flush at this stage you have a problem. In two discards you have a fair.chance of filling, roughly twice as good as drawing one card in Draw Poker. But in a Pot Limit game you may be asked to pay too heavy a price. Against one opponent who bets the limit now, and will presumably do the same after the first discard, you had best fold. If you have several opponents, or if no one is betting aggressively, then a straight or flush is worth pursuing.

After the bets have been equalized in this round of betting, you have to make the first discard. When you have a pair and also four cards to a straight or flush, split your pair if you suspect an opponent has a higher pair. You have as good a chance of improving and, more important, if you do improve you will probably win. However, the move is less sound if you have to split an open pair. You give away your intentiohs beyond the shadow of a doubt, and if your first discard doesn't help you, your opponent is going to make you pay heavily for a second chance.

In discarding from a pair, you occasionally get a minor problem over which card to throw. Normally choose the lowest, but discard any odd card, even an Ace or King, if you have seen others of the same denomination on the table. And if there is no particularly obvious choice, prefer to discard a useless up card than a useless down card so that you can take your last card face down.

4. *Fourth betting interval*, after the first discard. Much depends, of course, on what has gone before. If anybody has been at all aggressive, a pair is a very poor hand. But against a single opponent drawing to a straight or flush, a pair, especially a high pair, is an excellent hand. Opponents' chances of filling are no better than in Draw Poker. The importance of the exact denomination of your

own pair is simply that four-card straights or flushes can end up as a pair.

The discard after the fourth betting interval presents no new problems.

5. *Fifth and final betting interval*, after the second discard. By this time you should have a lot of information about any opponent. His bets, his discards and his up cards should add up to something definite. In any case, you can tell with absolute certainty the maximum possibilities of his hand. For instance, if he has three odd up cards which cannot be made into a straight or flush he cannot have better than triplets of his highest up card; and if you have accounted for two cards of that denomination elsewhere, then his maximum will be triplets of the next highest card. Your opponent, of course, has the same opportunity. He can gauge your maximum holding, and may know he has a cinch. As in straight Stud, you must beware of betting into possible cinches.

2. WITH A LOW LIMIT

Like most forms of poker, this game becomes rather different if played with a small limit. Keep more or less to the same standards in the early intervals, except that potential straights and flushes can be pursued with far more enthusiasm. You can soldier on to the last discard without getting badly out of line on percentages. With a pair and a four-card straight or flush at the fifth card, it is normally correct to split the pair and go for the flush or straight, the only exception being if you have a single opponent and he is himself aiming evidently at a straight or flush. In this case, keep your pair and make him pay the limit (such as it is) for the privilege of staying for the last two cards.

If you survive to the fifth card you will mostly be getting such good odds in chips that you should continue to the showdown if you have any chance at all of winning. In the final betting interval there may be possible cinches about, but the small limit deprives them of any great danger. If you think you have the best hand, always raise.

Bluff is difficult in a small-limit game, particularly in the end betting when the maximum bet may be only a small fraction of the total size of the pot. With a large limit there are often good opportunities. Suppose you start with ◇ 9 ♡ 9 in the hole and that after five or six cards you find yourself with ♣ 6 2 J on the table. If you stand pat and bet the limit, none but the brave will stay to the finish.

3. LOW ENGLISH STUD

This also is an excellent game, in our opinion the best low Stud Poker game there is. The laws are exactly the same except that the low hand wins. Aces count low.

The game requires rather less concentration than high Stud, as the inferences from the discards of other players are more evident. The general standard of final hands is better than in Lowball because of the one-by-one draw after the fifth card. Most pots are won by an eight high or better.

The general standards of play are as follows:

1. *First and second betting intervals*, after three and four cards. Stay if you have (*a*) the best hand showing, or (*b*) only one card higher than an eight, or (*c*) if discarding one card would give you a better hand than any showing. Raise with three good low cards in the first three or four good low cards in the first four unless an opponent is betting very aggressively.

2. *Third betting interval*, after the fifth card. Stay with a three-card eight only if the competition is not stiff and the price is small in relation to the pot. If no one is showing signs of activity, raise with a four-card eight.

3. *First discard*. Unless there is a formidable group of cards on the table reinforced by intensive betting in the early stages, stand pat with an eight high. As a rule, break up a nine high, especially if you can draw to a seven.

4. *Fourth betting interval*. In a small-limit game you will be getting such good odds that you can stay with almost any hopes. In

a large-limit game you have to be more cautious. Remember that drawing one card to an eight, you will on average end up as ten high, not a good hand in this game. Against someone who stood pat at the first discard, stay with an eight high, raise with a seven high. Against one or two opponents who are showing an up card higher than the nine, raise with a pat nine in an effort to protect your hand.

5. *Second discard.* At this point some knowledge of the chances of improvement is helpful. Against a single opponent who will have to discard, you should stand pat on a ten high. Against two opponents, you must aim for something better than a ten. Stand pat on a nine high unless you are sure you are beaten already.

6. *Fifth and final betting interval.* The player who has the best hand showing and acts first will often have a cinch. If so he should bet out. There is always a good chance of a call. His last card may have looked good, but there is always a doubt: it may have given him a pair or even a straight.

When the cards are all very low ones so that no one has an obvious cinch, you can, in a low-limit game, indulge in brinkmanship tactics based on mathematical probabilities. With a seven high, raise someone who stood pat at the first discard. With an eight high, raise someone who stood pat at the second discard. With an eight, or even a good nine, raise someone who took his last card face down. The chances are he has no better than a ten high. (These tactics would be overbold in a large-limit game where a slightly greater margin of probable superiority is required.)

You will often be able to judge that an opponent is not so formidable as he seems by recalling his betting on earlier rounds. For instance, if a player shows 2 4 6 and has neglected to raise at the first and second intervals, and has not since exchanged a down card, it is reasonable to suppose that he has a nine in the hole, for with three low cards he would have forced the pace from the outset.

It is perhaps difficult for a patriotic American to believe that the English could invent a good poker game, but whenever we have induced Americans to play the English form of Stud, they have liked it enormously. We have therefore thought it worthwhile to describe the game in some detail.

CHAPTER FOURTEEN

JOINING A POKER GAME

If a bridge player gets into a bridge game, he knows more or less what to expect. The players may be good or bad, but the form of the game and the laws under which it is played will be constant. There is no standard way of playing poker. The type of game, the rules, the etiquette, the stakes, will vary from game to game. Every poker group is unique and the game it plays is peculiar to itself. Therefore, before you join a new group, it is wise to do a certain amount of reconnoitering.

1. WHAT SORT OF A GAME IS IT?

The first thing you will want to know is the size of the game in terms of money. Any of the regulars in the group will tell you what is the maximum that anybody is likely to lose in an evening. This depends on the value of the chips, the ante, the limit, the kinds of poker played. Variations of Seven Card Stud, for example, produce larger pots than Straight Stud and much larger than Draw. As a very general rule, in a small-limit game, if the small chip is worth a cent, you will be unlucky to lose much more than $8.00. If the game is Pot Limit, you might lose $20. Note that there is not too much difference in the maximum probable loss. That is because in a large-limit game players bet far more cautiously.

Then you will want to know what variations are played. A staid, conservative game will confine itself to Jackpots, Lowball, Five Card Stud and Seven Card Stud. At the other extreme, the dealer in some games is virtually allowed to make his own rules. An off-beat group may play nothing but High-Low Stud.

Finally, you should kibitz the game for a while, to get the feel of it and to get a line on how the players bet. Observe the general character of the players. Do they bet freely or cautiously? No one minds a kibitzer, and one player will usually be quite willing to let you look at his hand during play. It would be unforgivable to look at someone else's hand as well during the play. You might give away information.

2. CUSTOMS AND ETHICS

Just as there are no official laws of poker, so also there is no official code of ethics, except the obvious rule that you must not cheat and must not form partnerships. However, there are some rules of behavior that are accepted as more or less binding, at least in any serious game.

1. When a player has dropped, don't ask him what he had, still less look at his discarded hand or turn up his hole card or cards.

2. Don't throw in your own hand out of turn. To do so may not make much difference to you, but it might benefit one player at the expense of another.

Example. "A" opens a Jackpot. "B" stays. You, sitting at "C," also stay. You draw one card to a flush and fail to fill. It is important that you should not throw in your hand until after "B" has acted. If you throw in before, and "A" checks and "B" raises, "A" has a legitimate complaint against you if he calls and loses. For with a one-card draw sitting over him, "B" might well have checked also.

3. Don't rabbit-hunt, that is, look through the undealt part of the pack to see what you would have drawn if you had stayed. It is distracting.

4. Don't try to give a misleading impression of your hand by deliberate acting. For instance, if you have an Ace in the hole, don't look at it constantly as if it was a nondescript card. If you have a pat six in Lowball, don't, when you are offered cards by the dealer, appear to ponder as though you had a pat nine or ten. This

sort of thing is known as coffee-housing and is highly disapproved of by poker players. Of course, there is no harm in the casual and flippant backchat that accompanies most games.

5. Strictly speaking, it is the chips put into the pot which make a bet, and a bet by word of mouth alone has no validity. But it wouldn't be very popular in most groups to try to take advantage of this rule.

6. At the showdown a player should state what he has, but it is the actual cards that count if he has made a mistake. This applies whether he has overstated or understated his hand.

7. At a showdown every player still in the game should expose his hand.

8. At Table Stakes everyone must keep his stack in a neat and orderly manner, so that the other players can tell at a glance roughly how many chips he has.

9. In Stud, the dealer should keep up a commentary on the hands, pointing out what they are and whether they are possible straights or flushes.

A curious facet of ethics is the attitude towards checking with a good hand and then re-raising if someone else bets. In some groups this is considered unfriendly. They think a check deprives one of the right to do anything more than call a subsequent bet. It seems illogical, for checking with a good hand is only a form of sandbagging and no one objects to that. But if you do find yourself in a group with these ideas you must conform to them, or you would be taking an unfair advantage and inviting unpopularity. You can easily overcome the difficulty if you bet one chip when you would otherwise have checked.

3. IRREGULARITIES IN DEAL AND PLAY

The usual customs regarding misdeals are as follows:

(*a*) If the dealer cannot correct a misdeal to the satisfaction of everyone there must be a fresh deal.

(*b*) If the dealer accidentally faces a card, it is put at the bottom of the pack and the next card is given in its place. If the dealer faces a second card, there must be a fresh deal.

(c) If a player picks up his cards and then discovers that he has an irregular number his hand is dead, but otherwise the game continues as usual.

(d) In Stud, if the dealer wrongly faces a card, that card is put at the bottom of the pack and the dealer continues to serve the following player. Finally he serves a down card to the player who missed his turn. In Seven Card Stud, if one of the first two cards of any player is faced, it is left where it is and the player receives his third card face down.

CHAPTER FIFTEEN

THE MATHEMATICS OF POKER AND HOW TO FIGURE PROBABILITIES AND ODDS

Every once in a while, you will find yourself in a poker game with a player who has a smattering of information about the mathematics of probabilities and odds in poker and who delights in demonstrating this knowledge.

This chapter is also intended for those poker players who are themselves curious about the mathematics of poker, either for the purpose of verifying the statistics spouted by the other players or for computing the probabilities or odds for themselves.

The mathematics of poker are not at all complicated. As a matter of fact, it is really not necessary to memorize any complicated tables of odds, for the exact odds and probabilities can be computed by anyone able to use simple arithmetic.

The rank of the various winning hands in poker, for example, is in inverse proportion to the chance of obtaining that particular hand. Assuming a normal 52-card deck with no jokers or wild cards, there are exactly 2,598,960 separate and different possible hands that could be dealt. (By contrast—in bridge there are 635,013,559,600 separate and different possible hands.)

The rank of the various hands in poker is based on the probability of that hand's turning up. Thus, there can be only 40 straight flushes, of which 4 are royal flushes (1 of each suit) and 36 are straight flushes other than royal. The chances of 4 royal flushes in 2,598,960 hands may be expressed as the fraction

$$\frac{2,598,960}{4} \quad \text{or}$$

1 in 649,765. Expressed as the odds against this happening, we say that for an individual player they are 649,764 to 1 against obtaining a royal flush on any deal.

The Mathematics of the Poker Hands

The following table summarizes the possibilities of being dealt any particular hand, the frequency of, and the odds against, that hand in Draw Poker:

Hand	No. Possible	Frequency	Odds Against
Royal flush	4	1 in 649,764	649,763 to 1
Straight flush below a royal	36	1 in 72,194	72,193 to 1
Straight flush including royal	40	1 in 64,974	64,973 to 1
Four of a kind	624	1 in 4,165	4,164 to 1
Full house	3,744	1 in 694	693 to 1
Flush	5,108	1 in 509	508 to 1
Straight	10,200	1 in 255	254 to 1
Three of a kind	54,912	1 in 47	46 to 1
Two pairs	123,522	1 in 21	20 to 1
One pair	1,098,240	1 in 2.4	1.4 to 1
No pair	1,302,540	1 in 1.99	0.9 to 1 (even)

The chances of getting any hand *or better* in the deal are given in the following table:

Hand		No. Possible	Frequency	Odds Against
Straight flush		40	1 in 64,974	64,973 to 1
Four of a kind or better		664	1 in 3,913	3,912 to 1
Full house	,, ,,	4,408	1 in 589	588 to 1
Flush	,, ,,	9,516	1 in 270	269 to 1
Straight	,, ,,	19,716	1 in 132	131 to 1
Three of a kind	,, ,,	74,628	1 in 35	34 to 1
Two pairs	,, ,,	198,180	1 in 13	12 to 1
Pair of Aces	,, ,,	282,660	1 in 9	8 to 1
Pair of Kings	,, ,,	367,140	1 in 7	6 to 1
Pair of Queens	,, ,,	451,620	1 in 6	5 to 1
Pair of Jacks	,, ,,	536,100	1 in 5	4 to 1
Any pair	,, ,,	1,500,720	1 in 1.7	0.7 to 1 (even)

The chances of drawing any *particular* pair are 1 in 31; the odds against this are 30 to 1. The reader should note the relationship between frequency and odds. Also, note that when the odds are said to be 4 to 1 against an event or 1 to 4 on an event, these are different ways of expressing the same thing—that there is a frequency of 1 in 5 of the event's happening.

One of the attractions of the game of poker is that it is based on mathematical principles. Three of a kind beats two pairs because the former is a rarer hand. These same mathematical principles can be applied to the play of a hand to determine whether to stay or fold, to bet or call. The odds and probabilities set out in this chapter can be readily computed by anyone who understands the general principles and method.

Computing Your Own Probabilities and Odds—Draw Poker

Every time you toss a coin, you have an equal chance of getting a head or a tail. It does not matter that you have tossed the coin ten times and gotten a head each time, your chances on the eleventh toss are exactly the same—1 in 2. The odds are 1 to 1 against getting either, or, in other words, your chances are even.

Similarly, when you receive your first card, your chances of getting a deuce are exactly the same as your chances of getting an Ace: 1 in 13. The odds against getting any particular denomination therefore are always 12 to 1 against. Of course, the chances of the second card's being anything in particular are different, being governed by the fact that certain cards have already been dealt and by the fact that you have one of them and have knowledge of what it is.

Nevertheless, it is possible for a player to compute probabilities and odds with reasonable exactness and to base his play on simple mental mathematical calculations that can be made without recourse to pencil and paper.

For example, you are in a tight Draw Poker game against careful players. You are dealt four hearts and a spade. You discard the spade and draw one card. What are the odds against making this a five-card flush? Disregard the cards held or discarded by the other players. The deck has 52 cards, you hold 4 of them and you have discarded 1. For calculation purposes, there are 47 cards outstanding. There are 13 hearts in a deck and you have accounted for four of them. The chances of getting a heart are exactly 9 in 47. The odds against getting a heart, therefore, are 38 to 9 against or 4.2 to 1 against.

Let us assume that you are dealt three tens, a King and a deuce. You discard the deuce and draw one card. What are your chances of making (a) four of a kind, (b) a full house, and (c) any improvement?

(a) There is only one ten outstanding in 47 cards. You have 1 chance in 47 cards. Therefore, you have 1 chance in 47 of making four of a kind; the odds against it are 46 to 1.

(b) To make a full house, you will need to draw a King. There are three Kings outstanding (the fact that these may already be tucked away in the hands of your opponents does not affect the mathematics of your calculations) among 47 cards. Your chances of drawing one of them are 3 in 47; the odds against are 44 to 3 or 14.7 to 1.

(c) To have *any* improvement you must draw either the fourth ten or one of the three outstanding Kings. Therefore, you have four chances in 47; your chances of drawing one of these are 43 to 4 or 10.8 to 1.

The following table shows the chances of improvement of 1-card draws:

ONE-CARD DRAWS

You hold	You draw	Objective	Odds Against
Two pairs	1 card	Full house	10.8 to 1
Three of a kind and a kicker	1 card	Four of a kind	46 to 1
		Full house	14.7 to 1
		Any improvement	10.8 to 1
Straight flush, open at either end	1 card	Straight flush	22.5 to 1
		Flush	4.2 to 1
		Straight	4.9 to 1
		Any improvement	2.1 to 1
Straight flush, open at one end or inside	1 card	Straight flush	46 to 1
		Flush	4.2 to 1
		Straight	10.8 to 1
		Any improvement	3 to 1
Four flush	1 card	Flush	4.2 to 1
Bobtail straight	1 card	Straight	4.9 to 1
Straight, open at one end or inside	1 card	Straight	10.8 to 1

The computation of the probabilities and odds involved in the drawing of two or more cards is somewhat more complicated. Mathematically, the probability that two or more independent events will occur is determined by multiplying the individual probabilities of each event. It is sometimes easier, however, to multiply together the individual probabilities of each event *not* taking place (i.e., multiplying the chances of failure) and subtracting this product from 1 to give the probability that two or more independent events will occur.

We have already investigated the chances of improving a hand consisting of three of a kind and a kicker. You hold three tens and discard a five and a deuce and draw two cards. What are your chances of making (*a*) four of a kind, (*b*) a full house, and (*c*) any improvements?

(*a*) You hold three of the tens; on the first card drawn, the chances against getting the fourth ten are 46 out of 47. On the second card drawn they are 45 out of 46.

The chances for the remaining ten on either card drawn thus are $\frac{46}{47} \times \frac{45}{46}$ or (cancelling and multiplying): $\frac{45}{47}$.

One minus $\frac{45}{47}$ equals $\frac{2}{47}$.

The chances of failure are 45 to 2 on, which means that it is 22.5 to 1 against drawing four of a kind.

Similarly the chances of making (*b*) a full house, and (*c*) any improvement, can be computed. The odds against making a full house are 15.4 to 1; against making any improvement they are 8.6 to 1.

The following table expresses some of the other odds against improvement in the draw:

TWO- AND THREE-CARD DRAWS

You hold	You draw	Objective	Odds Against
Any pair	3 cards	Four of a kind	359 to 1
		Full house	97 to 1
		Three of a kind	7.7 to 1
		Two pairs	5.3 to 1
		Any improvement	2.5 to 1
Any pair and ace kicker	2 cards	Four of a kind	1,080 to 1
		Full house	119 to 1
		Three of a kind	12 to 1
		Two pairs, Aces up	7.6 to 1
		Two pairs	17 to 1
		Any two pairs	4.8 to 1
		Any improvement	2.9 to 1
Three of a kind	2 cards	Four of a kind	22.5 to 1
		Full house	15.4 to 1
		Any improvement	8.6 to 1

One practical conclusion you will draw from this and the preceding table is that keeping a kicker in most cases reduces the chance of improvement. An exception is that keeping an Ace with a pair improves the chance of beating an opponent who holds two pairs. Apart from this, the usual reason for keeping a kicker is for variation or deception.

The following recapitulations illustrate the relative odds:

ODDS AGAINST MAKING

You hold	Any Improvement	2 Pairs	3 of a Kind	Full House	Four of a Kind
Any pair	2.5 to 1	5.3 to 1	7.7 to 1	97 to 1	359 to 1
Any pair and Ace kicker	2.9 to 1	4.8 to 1	12 to 1	119 to 1	1,080 to 1

Note that keeping a high kicker (Ace or King) with a pair gains only when the objective is to make two pairs.

ODDS AGAINST MAKING

You hold	Any Improvement	Full House	Four of a Kind
3 of a kind	8.6 to 1	15.4 to 1	22.5 to 1
3 of a kind and Ace kicker	10.8 to 1	14.7 to 1	46 to 1

Your chances of making a full house are somewhat improved by holding a kicker with three of a kind, but your chances of making four of a kind are halved.

The Mathematics of Two Pairs

There is a total of 123,552 hands comprised of two pairs, assuming Aces are high only. The following table shows the relative frequency of the various pairs:

Two Pairs	Total Possible	Total Possible Higher Two Pairs	Total Possible Lower Two Pairs
Aces up	19,008	0	104,544
K's up	17,424	19,008	87,120
Q's up	15,840	36,432	71,280
J's up	14,256	52,272	57,024
10's up	12,672	66,528	44,352
9's up	11,088	79,200	33,264
8's up	9,504	90,288	23,760
7's up	7,920	99,792	15,840
6's up	6,336	107,712	9,504
5's up	4,752	114,048	4,752
4's up	3,168	118,800	1,584
3's up	1,584	121,968	0

The important fact demonstrated by this table is the critical crossover point below two pairs, Jacks up. Below here the number of possible higher pairs exceeds the number of possible lower pairs. Therefore, if two pairs are betting against two pairs, or at least a hand suspected of containing two pairs, the odds are against a player who holds less than Jacks up.

Mathematics of Hands Containing Less Than One Pair

The following table shows the possibilities and odds against hands valued at less than one pair in the deal:

Hand	Odds Against
Ace high	4.2 to 1
King high	6.4 to 1
Queen high	11.2 to 1
Jack high	19.4 to 1
10 high	36 to 1
9 high	74 to 1
8 high	181 to 1
7 high	636 to 1

The Mathematics of Lowball

The chances of hands containing less than one pair winning in most poker games is slight. Therefore, the preceding table would have more significance for the game of Lowball. If the Ace is counted as a low card, the table becomes:

Hand	Odds Against
King high	4.2 to 1
Queen high	6.4 to 1
Jack high	11.2 to 1
10 high	19.4 to 1
9 high	36 to 1
8 high	74 to 1
7 high	181 to 1
6 high	636 to 1

(NOTE: These odds relate to genuine Lowball hands, not containing a straight or flush.)

The following table of hands less than one pair will be useful in California Lowball, where straights and flushes do not count:

Hand	Odds Against
9 high and better	19.1 to 1
8 " "	44.3 to 1
7 " "	120 to 1
6 " "	422 to 1
5 high (best hand)	2,537 to 1

The Mathematics of Stud Poker

The probabilities and odds in Five Card Stud Poker are exactly what they are in the deal in Draw Poker—with the exception that they are influenced by the cards shown on the board by the other players. Because there is more information available, the assessment of the odds has to be modified on the basis of the added information.

For example, you have been dealt 2 cards in a game of Five Card Stud. Your hole card is a high card and you want to know your chances of pairing that card. If no similar card shows elsewhere on the board, the odds against a card to match your hole card on the third card vary between 4 to 1 (seven-handed game) and 4.3 to 1 (five-handed game). If another card like your hole card shows elsewhere, the odds against your drawing still another on the third card vary between 5.4 to 1 (seven-handed game) and 5.8 to 1 (five-handed game).

The odds against pairing your hole card after the third card: With no similar card showing, they vary between 6.3 to 1 (seven-handed game or when opponents have a total of twelve cards showing) and 5.3 to 1 (five-handed game or when opponents have a total of 8 cards showing). With a card similar to your hole card showing, the odds against vary between 8.3 to 1 and 10 to 1 respectively.

If your first three cards are any pair and an odd card, the chances against improvement (i.e., two pairs, three of a kind, full house) are 2.5 to 1 if no card appears of the same denomination as the odd card and almost 3 to 1 against if there is another card showing on the board which is the same as either the pair or odd card.

The Mathematics of Poker with a Wild Joker

The addition of a joker to the ordinary 52-card deck makes for some slight adjustment in the total number of hands, their frequencies and the odds. The following table shows the changes (compare with table on page 114). There are now 2,869,685 possible hands:

Hand	No. Possible	Frequency	Odds Against
Five of a kind	13	1 in 220,745	220,744 to 1
Royal flush	24	1 in 119,570	119,569 to 1
Straight flush below royal	180	1 in 15,943	15,942 to 1
Straight flush including royal	204	1 in 14,067	14,066 to 1
Four of a kind	3,120	1 in 920	919 to 1
Full house	6,552	1 in 438	437 to 1
Flush	7,804	1 in 368	367 to 1
Straight	20,532	1 in 140	139 to 1
Three of a kind	137,280	1 in 21	20 to 1
Two pairs	123,552	1 in 23	22 to 1
One pair	1,268,088	1 in 2.3	1.3 to 1
No pair	1,302,540	1 in 2.2	1.2 to 1

The interesting fact revealed by this table, aside from the increased frequency of almost all hands (except hands less than one pair, which remain the same) and the addition of a new hand, five of a kind, is that three of a kind, formerly scarcer than two pairs, is now more frequent. This makes two pairs an even less likely winning hand than in Five-Card Stud or Draw Poker without the joker.

The Mathematics of Deuces Wild

Although giving the 4 deuces special powers does not change the *total* number of hands possible, it does drastically alter the order and frequency of the hands. Compare the following table with those on pages 114 and 123:

Hand	No. Possible	Frequency	Odds Against
Five of a kind	672	1 in 3,868	3,867 to 1
Royal flush	484	1 in 5,370	5,369 to 1
Straight flush below royal	4,072	1 in 638	637 to 1
Straight flush including royal	4,556	1 in 570	569 to 1
Four of a kind	30,816	1 in 84	83 to 1
Full house	12,672	1 in 205	204 to 1
Flush	13,204	1 in 197	196 to 1
Straight	66,236	1 in 39	38 to 1
Three of a kind	355,056	1 in 7	6 to 1
Two pairs	95,040	1 in 27	26 to 1
One pair	1,222,048	1 in 2.1	1.1 to 1
No pair	798,660	1 in 3.2	2.2 to 1

This table also reveals some interesting realignments: Five of a kind is much more difficult to get than a straight flush and accordingly ranks above it. Four of a kind is more common than either a flush or a straight and more common than the frequency of both together. Three of a kind will occur almost four times as frequently as two pairs, making it understandably the lowest playable hand.

THE LAWS OF POKER

There are no official Laws of Poker and wide divergencies in minor matters are to be found in different groups. We have attempted here to draw up a set of laws that follow the best usage and can be adapted to local variations.

We define correct procedure but have not set forth penalties for every kind of irregularity, as the attitude of different groups varies so much. The overriding principle in poker is that a player must pay for his own mistakes. If he speaks or plays or throws in out of turn, he cannot change his mind or retract his chips unless the bet has reached a higher level when his proper turn comes. He is responsible for looking after his own cards, for seeing that he gets the number of cards he asked for, and so forth.

1. GENERAL

Preliminaries

1. Poker is played with any number of players from five to seven and one pack of fifty-two cards. (In practice, two packs are used alternately.)

2. The game is divided into separate and distinct "hands" or "pots." All stakes go into the pot and are collected by the winner or, in certain cases, winners.

3. There are numerous varieties of poker, and it is for the players to decide which varieties are to be played and when. This may be according to some agreed cycle or the dealer may be allowed to choose the game.

4. Before beginning play the following must be decided:

    (*a*) The value of the chips.

    (*b*) The "ante," i.e., the amount to be staked compulsorily before the deal. It is recommended that the ante should be one chip from the dealer for Stud and two chips per player for Draw, plus one extra chip from the dealer.

125

(c) The "limit," i.e., the maximum amount of the opening bet and the maximum amount by which a previous bet can be raised.

The Deal

5. Any player starts dealing the pack and the first to receive a Jack becomes the first dealer. The deal subsequently passes to the left (clockwise) after each deal. The dealer must shuffle the pack himself and offer it for cutting to the player on his right. Other players have the right to shuffle before the dealer if they wish.

6. In the case of misdeals the following rules apply:
(a) In Draw Poker if more than one card is exposed during the deal there must be a redeal.
(b) The dealer adjusts any mistakes he can before the cards are picked up, but if any player picks up a hand with an incorrect number of cards his hand is "foul" or "dead." He cannot compete and cannot withdraw his ante.
(c) If a card is exposed during the draw, it is discarded and the player concerned is given another card after all the other players have drawn.
(d) In Stud, if an early hole card is exposed the player concerned gets his next card face down. If a final hole card is exposed it is discarded and that player gets a fresh hole card after all the other players.

Poker Hands

7. Poker hands consist of five cards and are ranked in the following order:
(a) Straight flush, a sequence of five cards in the same suit. An Ace can be used at the beginning or end of a sequence, e.g. ◇ A 2 3 4 5 ♣ 10 J Q K A. The latter example is the highest possible poker hand and is called a royal flush.

126

(b) Fours or four of a kind, four cards of one denomination and an odd card, e.g. 9 9 9 9 Q.

(c) Full house, three cards of one denomination and two of another, e.g., K K K 6 6. This example would be called a "full of Kings."

(d) Flush, any five cards of the same suit, e.g. ♠ K J 10 7 3.

(e) Straight, a sequence of five cards not all of the same suit, e.g. ◇ K 10 ♣ Q J ♡ 9. An Ace can be used at the beginning or end of a sequence, but not in the middle.

(f) Threes or three of a kind, three cards of one denomination and two odd cards, e.g. 7 7 7 K 4.

(g) Two pairs, e.g. Q Q 6 6 10. This example would be called "Queens up."

(h) A pair, e.g. 10 10 K 7 3.

(i) Five odd cards. If the highest card is a Queen, the hand is called "Queen high."

8. If two or more players show four of a kind, the highest four wins, the cards ranking in the order A K Q J 10 9 8 7 6 5 4 3 2.

9. If two or more players hold three of a kind, the highest threes win.

10. In the case of two straight flushes, or two flushes, or two straights, the hand with the highest card in it wins, except when an Ace is low in a straight. Suits are of equal rank in poker.

11. In the case of 2 two pairs, the highest pair wins. If these are the same, the next highest pair wins. If these are the same, the highest odd card wins.

12. In the case of two full houses, the highest three of a kind wins.

13. In the no pair category, the hand with the highest card wins. If these are the same, the next highest card determines the winner, and so on.

14. If two players hold exactly equal hands, they divide the pot.

2. STRAIGHT DRAW POKER

There are three varieties of this game, *Pass Out*, *Anything Opens* and *Blind and Straddle*.

PASS OUT

Before the Draw

15. All players put up the ante.

16. Five cards are dealt face down and one at a time to each player. Everyone picks up his hand and examines it.

17. The player on the left of the dealer is the first to act. He has the choice of "passing out," i.e., throwing in his hand, forfeiting his ante and taking no further part in the pot; or he can "open" by putting up one or more chips up to the agreed limit. If he throws in, the next player on the left has the same choice: He can pass out or open. If he passes, the next player has the same choice, and so on. If all pass in front of the dealer, the dealer wins the pot "unseen," i.e., without showing his hand, and collects the stakes, in this case only the antes.

18. If one player opens, the player on his left has the choice of (a) throwing in; or (b) staying in the game by "calling," i.e., putting up the same number of chips; or (c) "raising," i.e., putting up more chips but not exceeding the limit. Each player in turn has the choice of passing (throwing in his hand), calling the previous bet, or raising. The betting interval continues until all players have either passed or called the last raise. In the former case, the player who made the last raise wins the pot unseen, and collects all the stakes. In the latter case the draw takes place for those players who have stayed.

ANYTHING OPENS

19. In Anything Opens the first to speak after picking up his cards can open or pass (also called "check"), but if he checks he is allowed to "back in" later, i.e., he puts up his chips, but is entitled to call or raise if another player opens. Each player in turn has the same right until the pot is opened. The game then proceeds as already described. If all pass, there is a redeal by the same dealer.

The Draw

20. All those who have stayed are entitled to discard some or all of their cards and draw the same number of fresh cards with the object of improving their hands. They may also "stand pat" and draw no cards.

21. The dealer asks the player on his left, disregarding any intervening players who have thrown in, how many cards he wants. That player announces the number, places that number of cards face downwards on the table and receives from the top of the pack the same number of fresh cards. The dealer then gives cards to the next player, and so on. If the dealer has stayed, he must announce clearly the number of cards he is giving himself.

22. The dealer should not give the last card of the pack. If he runs out of cards, he shuffles the discards, has them cut and continues to give cards in the usual way.

After the Draw

23. The opener or, if the opener has thrown in, the next on his left, is the first to act after the draw. He can "check," i.e., put up no chips but reserve the right to call or raise if someone else bets, or he can bet by putting up any number of chips up to the limit.

24. If he checks, all other players have the same right, until one player makes a bet. If everyone checks, the "showdown" takes place. All players still in the pot place their hands face upward on the table, and the highest hand wins the pot.

25. If one player makes a bet, the others in rotation have the right to throw in, or to call by putting up the same amount as the previous bettor, or to raise. (The expression "see" is often used instead of "call.") The betting continues until all players have either thrown in or called the last raise. In the first case the player who made the raise that no one was willing to call wins the pot unseen. In the second case, the showdown takes place.

BLIND AND STRADDLE

This is the original form of poker. Little played in America today, it remains a standard game in England, Australia, and South Africa.

26. The player on the left of the dealer alone puts up an ante of one chip, known as the "blind." The player on his left can "straddle" by putting up twice the blind, i.e., two chips. The next player can "re-straddle" by putting up twice the straddle, i.e., four chips. (Usually the first straddle is compulsory, the re-straddle voluntary.) All this takes place before the deal or while the deal is going on.

27. All players look at their hands. The player on the left of the blind is the first to speak if there has been no straddling. Otherwise, the player on the left of the last straddle is first to speak. He has the choice of throwing in or opening for twice the blind, or twice the last straddle, as the case may be. Until a bet is made each player in turn has the same choice. If no one bets in front of the last to speak, he collects the blind and straddle, if any, and the hand is over.

28. If one player bets, the betting before the draw continues in the usual way. If the blind or straddle open or stay or raise they are required to put up only the difference between the required amount and the chips they have already contributed as a blind or straddle.

29. The draw and betting after the draw take place as already described.

130

3. JACKPOTS

This is probably played more than any other form of poker. Except for the restrictions on opening, the rules are exactly the same as for Anything Opens.

30. The ante and the deal take place in the usual way.

31. No player can open the pot unless he has a pair of Jacks or better. However, a player with legal openers is not obliged to open if he does not wish to.

32. The player on the left of the dealer either passes or opens by putting up any number of chips up to the limit. Until the pot is opened each player in turn has the same choice.

33. If no one opens, everyone "sweetens" the pot by putting in another chip, and the same dealer shuffles, has the pack cut and deals again.

34. As soon as one player opens, all the others in turn, including any who may have passed, have the usual choice of throwing in, staying or raising. The game proceeds as in Straight Draw.

35. After the draw the opener is first to act, or, if he threw in before the draw, the next on the left.

36. If the opener does not reach the showdown he must, if requested, show his openers.

37. The opener is entitled to split his openers by discarding one of his opening pair in order to draw to a straight or flush. He need not announce this at the time but he is responsible for keeping his discards available to prove, if requested, that he did have legal openers. (In some games the opener must announce when he is splitting openers.)

38. A player who opens illegally is not entitled to win the pot and forfeits all his chips staked. (He may also be required to pay some agreed penalty into the next pot.)

4. DEUCES WILD

39. The rules are as for Straight Draw (Anything Opens) except that all deuces (twos) are wild and can be used to represent any card in the pack. (The game can also be played under Jackpot rules.)

40. The new hand of five of a kind ranks above a straight flush. Thus, five Aces is the best possible hand. (In some schools a royal flush beats fives.)

41. The normal rules regarding equal hands apply. A joker has exactly the same value as a natural card. For example, if one player shows three Aces and another an Ace and two jokers, the next highest card will decide the issue. (A joker may also be considered inferior to a natural card.)

5. LOWBALL

42. The rules are as for Straight Draw (Anything Opens), except that the lowest hand wins instead of the highest.

43. Ace counts low. The lowest possible hand is therefore A 2 3 4 6, provided it is not a flush.

44. If two competing hands have equal high cards, the second cards decide the issue. For example, 9 7 6 5 4 will beat 9 8 4 3 2, assuming, of course, that neither hand is a flush.

6. SPIT IN THE OCEAN

45. Four cards are dealt in the usual way to each player, and finally one card face up in the center. This card, which is common to all hands, is wild and so are the other three cards of the same denomination. The game proceeds as in Straight Draw, i.e., there is an interval of betting, followed by the draw, followed by another interval of betting.

7. FIVE CARD STUD

This is the original form of Stud Poker and is still probably the most popular, particularly in serious gambling sessions.

46. One card is dealt face down and one card face up to each player. All look at their concealed or "hole" cards.

47. The holder of the highest exposed or "up" card makes the first bet. If two players show equal cards, the player nearest the dealer makes the first bet. A round of betting takes place in the usual manner. Players who throw in ("fold" is the usual expression in Stud) signify by turning their up card face down.

48. A third, fourth and fifth card is dealt to each player who stays, a round of betting taking place after each card. The highest exposed hand is first to bet. Checking is allowed in these betting intervals. (Checking is allowed in every round of betting except the first in most Stud games.)

49. The pot can be won unseen in any round of betting, or at a showdown after the fifth card and fourth betting interval.

8. SEVEN CARD STUD or DOWN THE RIVER

50. Two cards are dealt face down and four cards face up, an interval of betting taking place after each up card. The seventh and last card is dealt face down ("Down the River") followed by the fifth and final interval of betting.

51. At the showdown any five cards of the seven can be used to make up the best poker hand. The pot can also be won unseen, of course, in any betting interval.

9. ENGLISH STUD

52. Two cards are dealt face down and three cards face up, an interval of betting taking place after each up card.

53. The final two cards are dealt face up or face down according to whether a player uses them to replace an up or a down card. A

player may stand pat at the sixth or seventh card. If he stands pat at the sixth he must also stand pat at the seventh card. An interval of betting takes place after the sixth and seventh cards have been given or offered. There are therefore five intervals of betting, and each player who reaches the showdown will have two hole cards and three up cards.

10. BASEBALL

54. The rules are as for Down the River with the following additions:

(a) All nines are wild.

(b) A player who receives an exposed three must pay a penalty of half the pot into the pot if he wishes to stay. If he does this, all threes become wild. (The penalty can be less or more. It should be fairly large since the whole point of the game is the uncertainty whether there are going to be four wild cards or eight.)

(c) A player who receives an exposed four has the option of discarding it immediately and getting the next card in its place.

11. CINCINNATI

55. Five cards are dealt to each player as in Draw Poker, and five extra are dealt face down in the center of the table. The center cards are turned up one at a time, an interval of betting taking place after each card. Each player makes the best poker hand he can out of his own and the center cards.

12. LOW STUD POKER

56. Any form of Stud Poker can be played with the low hand winning. (Five Card Stud and English Stud make the best games.)

13. HIGH-LOW POKER

57. The rules are as for Straight Draw Poker or Five Card Stud, or English Stud, or Down the River, or Cincinnati, but the pot is divided between the highest and the lowest hand.

58. If two players have exactly equal hands they divide that half of the pot between them.

59. In High-Low Seven Card Stud (Down the River) each player has in effect two hands and can win both high and low. For instance 2 3 4 5 6 7 K can be counted as a seven low and a straight. The same sort of thing can happen in Cincinnati. (Sometimes the game is played "Contract" and each player, before he makes his bet in the last betting interval, must declare whether he is going high, low or both ways. If he declares both ways he is not entitled to collect half the pot if he only wins one way. He wins all or nothing.)

14. POKER WITH THE BUG

60. Any form of poker can be played with a pack of fifty-three cards, the fifty-third card being a joker with limited powers known as the Bug. It can be used as an Ace or as part of a straight or flush or straight flush.

15. OTHER GAMES

See Chapter 11 for the rules governing the following variations:

Mexican Stud or Flip	Doctor Pepper
New York Stud	Low Hole Card Wild
Shifting Sands	Kankakee
Woolworth	Bedsprings
Football	Cincinnati Liz

GLOSSARY

We have included in this glossary a brief description of certain games such as Kankakee and Cincinnati Liz, even though these games are described in the text. We have not thought it necessary to include in the glossary games like Seven Card Stud, whose very title is self-explanatory.

We include also a number of "not-real-poker" hands that in some schools are given a rating in certain variants of the game.

Active player. A player who is still competing in the pot.

Age. An obsolete term meaning the player on the left of the dealer. Also known as the *Edge*.

Alternate straight. A straight comprised of every other card; not a standard hand. Example: 10, 8, 6, 4, 2; 9, 7, 5, 3, A. It beats three of a kind and loses to a straight. (Also called a *Dutch straight*, *skip straight*, or *skipper*.)

Ante. Chips staked compulsorily before the deal. The first bet by the player to the left of the dealer in Straight Draw Poker.

Around the corner straight. A straight with an Ace anywhere but at either end; not a standard hand. Example 3 2 A K Q. It beats an ordinary straight, but loses to a flush.

Back in. To come into a pot having previously checked. This is allowed in all forms of Draw Poker that are not played Pass Out.

Back-to-back. When the hole card and the first up card in Five Card Stud are the same, they are said to be, say, Aces back-to-back or Aces wired.

Banker. The player in charge of the chips.

Baseball. A version of Seven Card Stud with all nines wild and special penalties for threes and special options for fours.

Beat the table or *Beat the board.* To beat all other hands showing.

Bedsprings. A variant of Cincinnati, in which five cards are dealt to each player and ten are dealt face down in the center.

Bet. Loosely, any chips put into the pot. Strictly, the first bet in any round of betting.

Bet blind. To bet before you have looked at your cards.

Bet into. To bet ahead of another player whose open cards, bets or draw indicate that his hand may be better.

Bet the limit. To bet the agreed maximum amount permitted.

Bet the raise. A bet limit that permits a player to raise by an amount equivalent to the maximum bet by another player.

Betting interval. The period in which each active player has the chance of betting or folding.

Betty Hutton. A version of Seven Card Stud with nines and fives wild.

Big bobtail. A four-card straight flush; not a standard hand. It beats a full house and loses to four of a kind.

Big cat. King high, eight low, with no pair nor a flush; not a standard hand. It beats a straight and loses to a flush. Also sometimes called *Big tiger.*

Big dog. Ace high, nine low, with no pair nor a flush; not a standard hand. It beats a straight, loses to both cats.

Big squeeze. Six Card, High-Low Stud with one draw.

Big tiger. See *Big cat.*

Blaze. A hand of five picture cards including two pairs; not a standard hand. It beats Aces up and loses to triplets. In some games, it beats a flush and a Blaze full beats Aces full.

Blind. The ante put up by the player on the dealer's left in one form of Draw Poker. Also the player who opens blind.

Bluff. A bet on a hand that couldn't win in a showdown.

Bobtail. A four-card, open-ended straight.

Bones. Chips.

Bonus. In some games, exceptional hands exact a penalty from each player.

Buck. A marker sometimes used to indicate what game is being played. Originally a knife with a buckhorn handle that was won with a Draw Poker pot. When it was the turn of the winner of the buck to deal, he could either pass it to the player to his left or put the buck in the pot and choose the variation of poker he would deal. The winner of the pot (and of the buck) had the same option. The phrase "to pass the buck" is derived from this.

Bug. A joker which can only be used as an Ace or as part of a straight or flush.

Burnt card. A card wrongly exposed in the deal; in Stud usually replaced by the third card from the bottom of the deck.

Busted flush. A four flush that didn't fill.

Buy. Cards received in the draw. To pay for the privilege of drawing cards.

By me. Can mean "I pass" or "I want no cards."

California Lowball. Lowball, in which straights and flushes do not count and 5 4 3 2 A is the lowest hand.

Call. To put up the same number of chips as the previous bettor and to "see" the last bet made.

Canadian Stud. A variant of Five Card Stud in which a four flush beats a pair. Also called *New York Stud.*

Carding. Noting the cards which are exposed in Stud and drawing conclusions from them.

Cash in. To withdraw from a game.

Check. To put up no chips but to reserve the right to call or raise if someone else bets. To make a bet of nothing.

Chicago. A variant of Seven Card Stud in which the highest spade wins one-half the pot.

Chip. Discs used for betting in poker. The expression "to chip in" probably originated in poker.

Choice pot. A pot in which the dealer can choose the game.

Cinch. An unbeatable hand. An immortal. A lock.

Cincinnati. A mixture of Stud and Draw Poker; five cards are dealt and there is also a widow hand of five cards in the center with a round of betting after each of the center cards are turned up.

Cincinnati Liz. A variant of Cincinnati in which the lowest card in the center and its mates are wild.

Come in. To stay. To call. To play.

Cut. After the cards have been shuffled, the deck is divided into two or more parts and the lower part or parts are placed on top.

Dead hand. A hand which may not compete. Also used for the hand of a player who has been tapped at Table Stakes.

Dead man's hand. Two pairs, Aces and eights. So called because it is supposed to have been the hand held by Wild Bill Hickok in Deadwood when he was shot by Jack McCall in 1876.

Deal. To distribute cards to the players one at a time.

Dealer's choice. The dealer is allowed to choose the game.

Dealer's percentage. See *Little Squeeze.*

Deuce. A two. A two-spot.

Deuces Wild. A game in which the twos can stand for any other card.

Discard. Cards discarded in Draw Poker or in English Stud.

Dr. Pepper. Seven Card Stud Poker with tens, fours and twos wild.

Double. Literally, to double the last bet. It has come to mean "bet the limit."

Down the River. Another name for Seven Card Stud.

Draw. To receive fresh cards after the first betting interval in Draw Poker.

Draw Poker. One of the oldest versions of the game in which players may discard cards received in the deal and draw an equal number from the deck in the hope of improving their hands.

Drop. To throw in, to fold, to pass out.

Dutch straight. See alternate straight.

Edge. The age, which see.

End betting. Betting in the last interval.

English Stud. Sometimes called poker with options. See Chapter 13.

Exposed card. An up card in Stud.

Feed the kitty. To sweeten the pot by putting in more chips before the deal.

Fill. To complete a full house or a flush or a straight.

Flash. 4 suits and a joker; not a standard hand. Beats two pairs and loses to three of a kind.

Flip. See *Mexican Stud*.

Flush. A hand of five cards of the same suit.

Fold. To drop in Stud. To throw in, to pass out.

Football. Seven Card Stud Poker with sixes and fours wild.

Four flush. Four cards of the same suit. The term "four flusher" has come to mean a bluffer or a pretender, because of the temptation to pretend that the flush has been filled. In New York or Canadian Stud, it beats a pair.

Four of a kind. Fours. Four cards of the same denomination and an odd card.

Freak. A joker. A wild card which can be used to represent any card in the pack.

Freeze out. An old-fashioned form of Table Stakes in which a player who loses his takeout must retire.

Full house. Three of a kind and a pair.

Game. Any variant of poker. Is also used in the general sense.

Half-pot limit. A player may not bet or raise more than an amount equal to half the size of the pot.

Hand. The cards dealt to and drawn by a player.

Heinz. Seven Card Stud with fives and sevens wild.

High-Low. Variations of poker in which the best high hand and the "best" low hand split the pot.

High-Low Baseball. A variant of baseball with high and low hands winning half of the pot.

Hole card. A down card in Stud.

Immortal. A cinch. An unbeatable hand.

Inside straight. A four-card straight with the missing card inside, not at either end.

Iron Cross. A variant of Cincinnati, with nine cards dealt in the center. Players may use the cards in either the horizontal or the vertical row to augment the cards in their hands. Also called *Southern Cross*.

Jackpots. A variant of Draw Poker in which a pair of Jacks or better is required to open the betting.

Jacks Back. A variant of Draw Poker in which the deal starts out as Jackpots; if no one opens the game reverts to Lowball without a re-deal. Also called *Jackson* or *Jacks and Reverse*.

Joker. Any wild card added to the deck.

Kankakee. A variant of Seven Card Stud with a card dealt face up in the center, which is wild and common to all hands.

Kicker. In Draw Poker an odd card retained with a pair or threes in the hope of bettering the hand on the draw.

Kilter. Also called *Pelter*, *Skeet*, etc. A special hand varying locally. For example, a hand containing 9 5 2 and no other cards between the 9 and 5 and 5 and 2. It beats three of a kind and loses to a straight.

Kitty. A special fund belonging to all players built up by taking a fixed amount out of every pot.

Light. Chips owed by a player to be repaid after the showdown. Example, "I'm light five chips."

Limit. The maximum size of a bet or raise.

Little bobtail. A three-card straight flush; not a standard hand. It beats two pairs and loses to three of a kind.

Little cat. Eight high, three low, with no pair nor a flush; not a standard hand. It beats a straight, loses to a Big cat. (Also sometimes called *Little Tiger*.)

Little dog. Seven high, two low, with no pair nor a flush; not a standard hand. It beats a straight and loses to both cats and Big dog. This happens to be the lowest winning hand in Lowball.

Little Squeeze. High-Low Five Card Stud with a draw.

Lock. A cinch hand.

Lowball. A form of Draw Poker in which values are reversed—what is normally the worst hand winning the pot. Also called *Misère*.

Mexican Stud. A variant of Five Card Stud in which an optional hole card (two are dealt) and all matching open cards are wild. Also called *Flip* or *Peep and Turn*.

Misère. See *Lowball*.

Miss out. To fail to improve any hand in the draw as expected.

Monkey flush. A three-card flush.

Natural. A hand containing no wild cards; any winning hand that does not depend on wild cards.

New York Stud. A variant of Five Card Stud in which a four flush beats a pair. Also called *Canadian Stud*.

One-eyed Jacks. The Jack of hearts and the Jack of spades. So called because they are seen in profile. Only the King of diamonds is one-eyed; none of the Queens are one-eyed.

Open. To make the first bet after the ante.

Openers. Cards required to open in certain forms of poker, e.g., in Jackpots.

Open pair. An exposed pair in Stud.

Overlays. Cards in Stud which are higher in rank than an open pair.

Pair. Two cards of the same rank in a hand.

Pass. To throw in, to withdraw from the deal.

Pass Out. A form of Straight Draw Poker in which a player must open with a bet or throw in his hand.

Pat hand. A hand with which the owner does not elect to draw any cards.

Peep and turn. See *Mexican Stud*.

Pelter. See *Kilter*.

Pot. All the stakes in any one deal. Also used to describe a game in which all the players put up an equal ante, as opposed to Blind and Straddle where only certain players ante.

Pot limit. A player may always bet or raise an amount equivalent to the size of the pot.

Raise. To put up more chips than the previous bettor.

Restraddle. To put up twice the amount of the straddle.

Roodle. A hand played for increased stakes.

Round. A cycle of one deal from each player.

Royal flush. A K Q J 10 in one suit. Often abbreviated to "Royal." Sometimes also used to mean the best possible hand in Lowball, 6 4 3 2 A.

Run. A straight or sequence.

Sandbag. To check with a good hand, raising later after someone has opened.

See. To call in the last betting interval.

Shifting Sands. A variant of Mexican Stud. Players choose a wild card from their two hole cards. All cards of that rank in the player's hand are wild.

Shotgun. A variant of Straight Draw Poker in which there is predraw betting after the third, fourth and fifth cards have been dealt. This results in larger pots.

Showdown. If the last bet in the last betting interval is called, the players concerned put their hands face up on the table in Draw or turn up their hole cards in Stud, and the best hand wins the pot. Also a game in which five cards are dealt face up; the best hand wins. Usually played to divide up an amount of money remaining.

Shy. Having failed to put the correct number of chips into the pot.

Six Card Stud. Dealt as in Five Card Stud with the sixth card down.

Skeet. See *Kilter.*

Splitting Openers. Discarding one or more cards of your opening requirements in Jackpots.

Squeeze. Betting into a one-card draw or a possible cinch in Stud with a view to scaring out intervening players.

Stack. Pile of chips. Takeout.

Stand pat. To draw no cards. To decline to discard in English Stud.

Stay. To call in early rounds of betting. To come in. To play.

Straddle. To put up twice the amount of the Blind in one form of poker.

Straight. A sequence of five cards in more than one suit.

144

Straight Draw Poker. A pot in which there are no opening requirements.

Straight flush. A sequence of five cards in the same suit.

Straight Poker. The original form of poker without the draw. Also used to denote Straight Draw Poker, as opposed to Jackpots, etc.

Stripped deck. A deck with the twos, threes and fours removed. Often used for games involving a small number of players.

Stud. Any variant of poker in which some cards are dealt face down and others open, or face up.

Sweeten the pot. To put an additional ante into the pot if it is not opened.

Table Stakes. A form of limit in which no player may bet more than he actually has in front of him on the table.

Takeout. The stack of chips which each player starts off with at Table Stakes.

Tap. To bet your whole stack in Table Stakes or to make a bet which compels another player to bet his whole stack if he wants to call.

Three of a kind. E.g., 10 10 10 K 2. Also called *Threes* or *Triplets*.

Trey. A three.

Triplets. Three of a kind.

Two pairs. A hand containing two pairs of different rank and a fifth card.

Under the guns. Player on the left of the dealer, or the first to speak, in Draw Poker.

Up card. Any exposed card in Stud.

Wheel. The 5 4 3 2 A of any suit. So called because it is a hand shown on one of a particular brand of playing cards.

Widow. Card or cards that are common to all hands, as in Cincinnati or Spit in the Ocean.

Wild card. A card that can be used to represent any card; see also the *Bug*.

Wired. When the hole card and the first up card are the same in Five Card Stud they are said to be "wired" or "back to back."

Woolworth. A hand of any five cards from a ten down to a five with no paired cards and no flush; not a standard hand. It beats three of a kind and loses to any hand that beats three of a kind. Also Seven Card Stud with all fives and tens wild.

INDEX

A PERSONAL WORD FROM MELVIN POWERS
PUBLISHER, WILSHIRE BOOK COMPANY

Dear Friend:

My goal is to publish interesting, informative, and inspirational books. You can help me accomplish this by answering the following questions, either by phone or by mail. Or, if convenient for you, I would welcome the opportunity to visit with you in my office and hear your comments in person.

Did you enjoy reading this book? Why?

Would you enjoy reading another similar book?

What idea in the book impressed you the most?

If applicable to your situation, have you incorporated this idea in your daily life?

Is there a chapter that could serve as a theme for an entire book? Please explain.

If you have an idea for a book, I would welcome discussing it with you. If you already have one in progress, write or call me concerning possible publication. I can be reached at (213) 875-1711 or (818) 983-1105.

Sincerely yours,

MELVIN POWERS

12015 Sherman Road
North Hollywood, California 91605

MELVIN POWERS SELF-IMPROVEMENT LIBRARY

ASTROLOGY
_____ ASTROLOGY: HOW TO CHART YOUR HOROSCOPE *Max Heindel*	3.00
_____ ASTROLOGY: YOUR PERSONAL SUN-SIGN GUIDE *Beatrice Ryder*	3.00
_____ ASTROLOGY FOR EVERYDAY LIVING *Janet Harris*	2.00
_____ ASTROLOGY MADE EASY *Astarte*	3.00
_____ ASTROLOGY MADE PRACTICAL *Alexandra Kayhle*	3.00
_____ ASTROLOGY, ROMANCE, YOU AND THE STARS *Anthony Norvell*	4.00
_____ MY WORLD OF ASTROLOGY *Sydney Omarr*	5.00
_____ THOUGHT DIAL *Sidney Omarr*	4.00
_____ WHAT THE STARS REVEAL ABOUT THE MEN IN YOUR LIFE *Thelma White*	3.00

BRIDGE
_____ BRIDGE BIDDING MADE EASY *Edwin B. Kantar*	7.00
_____ BRIDGE CONVENTIONS *Edwin B. Kantar*	7.00
_____ BRIDGE HUMOR *Edwin B. Kantar*	5.00
_____ COMPETITIVE BIDDING IN MODERN BRIDGE *Edgar Kaplan*	4.00
_____ DEFENSIVE BRIDGE PLAY COMPLETE *Edwin B. Kantar*	10.00
_____ GAMESMAN BRIDGE—Play Better with Kantar *Edwin B. Kantar*	5.00
_____ HOW TO IMPROVE YOUR BRIDGE *Alfred Sheinwold*	5.00
_____ IMPROVING YOUR BIDDING SKILLS *Edwin B. Kantar*	4.00
_____ INTRODUCTION TO DECLARER'S PLAY *Edwin B. Kantar*	5.00
_____ INTRODUCTION TO DEFENDER'S PLAY *Edwin B. Kantar*	3.00
_____ KANTAR FOR THE DEFENSE *Edwin B. Kantar*	5.00
_____ SHORT CUT TO WINNING BRIDGE *Alfred Sheinwold*	3.00
_____ TEST YOUR BRIDGE PLAY *Edwin B. Kantar*	5.00
_____ VOLUME 2—TEST YOUR BRIDGE PLAY *Edwin B. Kantar*	5.00
_____ WINNING DECLARER PLAY *Dorothy Hayden Truscott*	5.00

BUSINESS, STUDY & REFERENCE
_____ CONVERSATION MADE EASY *Elliot Russell*	3.00
_____ EXAM SECRET *Dennis B. Jackson*	3.00
_____ FIX-IT BOOK *Arthur Symons*	2.00
_____ HOW TO DEVELOP A BETTER SPEAKING VOICE *M. Hellier*	3.00
_____ HOW TO MAKE A FORTUNE IN REAL ESTATE *Albert Winnikoff*	4.00
_____ INCREASE YOUR LEARNING POWER *Geoffrey A. Dudley*	3.00
_____ PRACTICAL GUIDE TO BETTER CONCENTRATION *Melvin Powers*	3.00
_____ PRACTICAL GUIDE TO PUBLIC SPEAKING *Maurice Forley*	5.00
_____ 7 DAYS TO FASTER READING *William S. Schaill*	3.00
_____ SONGWRITERS' RHYMING DICTIONARY *Jane Shaw Whitfield*	5.00
_____ SPELLING MADE EASY *Lester D. Basch & Dr. Milton Finkelstein*	3.00
_____ STUDENT'S GUIDE TO BETTER GRADES *J. A. Rickard*	3.00
_____ TEST YOURSELF—Find Your Hidden Talent *Jack Shafer*	3.00
_____ YOUR WILL & WHAT TO DO ABOUT IT *Attorney Samuel G. Kling*	4.00

CALLIGRAPHY
_____ ADVANCED CALLIGRAPHY *Katherine Jeffares*	7.00
_____ CALLIGRAPHER'S REFERENCE BOOK *Anne Leptich & Jacque Evans*	7.00
_____ CALLIGRAPHY—The Art of Beautiful Writing *Katherine Jeffares*	7.00
_____ CALLIGRAPHY FOR FUN & PROFIT *Anne Leptich & Jacque Evans*	7.00
_____ CALLIGRAPHY MADE EASY *Tina Serafini*	7.00

CHESS & CHECKERS
_____ BEGINNER'S GUIDE TO WINNING CHESS *Fred Reinfeld*	4.00
_____ CHESS IN TEN EASY LESSONS *Larry Evans*	5.00
_____ CHESS MADE EASY *Milton L. Hanauer*	3.00
_____ CHESS PROBLEMS FOR BEGINNERS *edited by Fred Reinfeld*	2.00
_____ CHESS SECRETS REVEALED *Fred Reinfeld*	2.00
_____ CHESS STRATEGY—An Expert's Guide *Fred Reinfeld*	2.00
_____ CHESS TACTICS FOR BEGINNERS *edited by Fred Reinfeld*	4.00
_____ CHESS THEORY & PRACTICE *Morry & Mitchell*	2.00
_____ HOW TO WIN AT CHECKERS *Fred Reinfeld*	3.00
_____ 1001 BRILLIANT WAYS TO CHECKMATE *Fred Reinfeld*	4.00
_____ 1001 WINNING CHESS SACRIFICES & COMBINATIONS *Fred Reinfeld*	4.00

___ SOVIET CHESS *Edited by R. G. Wade*		3.00

COOKERY & HERBS

___ CULPEPER'S HERBAL REMEDIES *Dr. Nicholas Culpeper*		3.00
___ FAST GOURMET COOKBOOK *Poppy Cannon*		2.50
___ GINSENG The Myth & The Truth *Joseph P. Hou*		3.00
___ HEALING POWER OF HERBS *May Bethel*		4.00
___ HEALING POWER OF NATURAL FOODS *May Bethel*		3.00
___ HERB HANDBOOK *Dawn MacLeod*		3.00
___ HERBS FOR COOKING AND HEALING *Dr. Donald Law*		2.00
___ HERBS FOR HEALTH—How to Grow & Use Them *Louise Evans Doole*		3.00
___ HOME GARDEN COOKBOOK—Delicious Natural Food Recipes *Ken Kraft*		3.00
___ MEDICAL HERBALIST *edited by Dr. J. R. Yemm*		3.00
___ NATURAL FOOD COOKBOOK *Dr. Harry C. Bond*		3.00
___ NATURE'S MEDICINES *Richard Lucas*		3.00
___ VEGETABLE GARDENING FOR BEGINNERS *Hugh Wiberg*		2.00
___ VEGETABLES FOR TODAY'S GARDENS *R. Milton Carleton*		2.00
___ VEGETARIAN COOKERY *Janet Walker*		4.00
___ VEGETARIAN COOKING MADE EASY & DELECTABLE *Veronica Vezza*		3.00
___ VEGETARIAN DELIGHTS—A Happy Cookbook for Health *K. R. Mehta*		2.00
___ VEGETARIAN GOURMET COOKBOOK *Joyce McKinnel*		3.00

GAMBLING & POKER

___ ADVANCED POKER STRATEGY & WINNING PLAY *A. D. Livingston*		5.00
___ HOW NOT TO LOSE AT POKER *Jeffrey Lloyd Castle*		3.00
___ HOW TO WIN AT DICE GAMES *Skip Frey*		3.00
___ HOW TO WIN AT POKER *Terence Reese & Anthony T. Watkins*		5.00
___ SECRETS OF WINNING POKER *George S. Coffin*		3.00
___ WINNING AT CRAPS *Dr. Lloyd T. Commins*		4.00
___ WINNING AT GIN *Chester Wander & Cy Rice*		3.00
___ WINNING AT POKER—An Expert's Guide *John Archer*		5.00
___ WINNING AT 21—An Expert's Guide *John Archer*		5.00
___ WINNING POKER SYSTEMS *Norman Zadeh*		3.00

HEALTH

___ BEE POLLEN *Lynda Lyngheim & Jack Scagnetti*		3.00
___ DR. LINDNER'S SPECIAL WEIGHT CONTROL METHOD *P. G. Lindner, M.D.*		2.00
___ HELP YOURSELF TO BETTER SIGHT *Margaret Darst Corbett*		3.00
___ HOW TO IMPROVE YOUR VISION *Dr. Robert A. Kraskin*		3.00
___ HOW YOU CAN STOP SMOKING PERMANENTLY *Ernest Caldwell*		3.00
___ MIND OVER PLATTER *Peter G. Lindner, M.D.*		3.00
___ NATURE'S WAY TO NUTRITION & VIBRANT HEALTH *Robert J. Scrutton*		3.00
___ NEW CARBOHYDRATE DIET COUNTER *Patti Lopez-Pereira*		2.00
___ QUICK & EASY EXERCISES FOR FACIAL BEAUTY *Judy Smith-deal*		2.00
___ QUICK & EASY EXERCISES FOR FIGURE BEAUTY *Judy Smith-deal*		2.00
___ REFLEXOLOGY *Dr. Maybelle Segal*		3.00
___ REFLEXOLOGY FOR GOOD HEALTH *Anna Kaye & Don C. Matchan*		3.00
___ YOU CAN LEARN TO RELAX *Dr. Samuel Gutwirth*		3.00
___ YOUR ALLERGY—What To Do About It *Allan Knight, M.D.*		3.00

HOBBIES

___ BEACHCOMBING FOR BEGINNERS *Norman Hickin*		2.00
___ BLACKSTONE'S MODERN CARD TRICKS *Harry Blackstone*		3.00
___ BLACKSTONE'S SECRETS OF MAGIC *Harry Blackstone*		3.00
___ COIN COLLECTING FOR BEGINNERS *Burton Hobson & Fred Reinfeld*		3.00
___ ENTERTAINING WITH ESP *Tony 'Doc' Shiels*		2.00
___ 400 FASCINATING MAGIC TRICKS YOU CAN DO *Howard Thurston*		4.00
___ HOW I TURN JUNK INTO FUN AND PROFIT *Sari*		3.00
___ HOW TO WRITE A HIT SONG & SELL IT *Tommy Boyce*		7.00
___ JUGGLING MADE EASY *Rudolf Dittrich*		3.00
___ MAGIC FOR ALL AGES *Walter Gibson*		4.00
___ MAGIC MADE EASY *Byron Wels*		2.00
___ STAMP COLLECTING FOR BEGINNERS *Burton Hobson*		3.00

HORSE PLAYERS' WINNING GUIDES

___ BETTING HORSES TO WIN *Les Conklin*		3.00
___ ELIMINATE THE LOSERS *Bob McKnight*		3.00

____ HOW TO PICK WINNING HORSES *Bob McKnight*	3.00
____ HOW TO WIN AT THE RACES *Sam (The Genius) Lewin*	5.00
____ HOW YOU CAN BEAT THE RACES *Jack Kavanagh*	3.00
____ MAKING MONEY AT THE RACES *David Barr*	3.00
____ PAYDAY AT THE RACES *Les Conklin*	3.00
____ SMART HANDICAPPING MADE EASY *William Bauman*	3.00
____ SUCCESS AT THE HARNESS RACES *Barry Meadow*	3.00
____ WINNING AT THE HARNESS RACES—An Expert's Guide *Nick Cammarano*	5.00

HUMOR

____ HOW TO BE A COMEDIAN FOR FUN & PROFIT *King & Laufer*	2.00
____ HOW TO FLATTEN YOUR TUSH *Coach Marge Reardon*	2.00
____ HOW TO MAKE LOVE TO YOURSELF *Ron Stevens & Joy Grdnic*	3.00
____ JOKE TELLER'S HANDBOOK *Bob Orben*	3.00
____ JOKES FOR ALL OCCASIONS *Al Schock*	3.00
____ 2000 NEW LAUGHS FOR SPEAKERS *Bob Orben*	4.00
____ 2,500 JOKES TO START 'EM LAUGHING *Bob Orben*	4.00

HYPNOTISM

____ ADVANCED TECHNIQUES OF HYPNOSIS *Melvin Powers*	3.00
____ BRAINWASHING AND THE CULTS *Paul A. Verdier, Ph.D.*	3.00
____ CHILDBIRTH WITH HYPNOSIS *William S. Kroger, M.D.*	5.00
____ HOW TO SOLVE Your Sex Problems with Self-Hypnosis *Frank S. Caprio, M.D.*	5.00
____ HOW TO STOP SMOKING THRU SELF-HYPNOSIS *Leslie M. LeCron*	3.00
____ HOW TO USE AUTO-SUGGESTION EFFECTIVELY *John Duckworth*	3.00
____ HOW YOU CAN BOWL BETTER USING SELF-HYPNOSIS *Jack Heise*	3.00
____ HOW YOU CAN PLAY BETTER GOLF USING SELF-HYPNOSIS *Jack Heise*	3.00
____ HYPNOSIS AND SELF-HYPNOSIS *Bernard Hollander, M.D.*	3.00
____ HYPNOTISM *(Originally published in 1893)* *Carl Sextus*	5.00
____ HYPNOTISM & PSYCHIC PHENOMENA *Simeon Edmunds*	4.00
____ HYPNOTISM MADE EASY *Dr. Ralph Winn*	3.00
____ HYPNOTISM MADE PRACTICAL *Louis Orton*	3.00
____ HYPNOTISM REVEALED *Melvin Powers*	2.00
____ HYPNOTISM TODAY *Leslie LeCron and Jean Bordeaux, Ph.D.*	5.00
____ MODERN HYPNOSIS *Lesley Kuhn & Salvatore Russo, Ph.D.*	5.00
____ NEW CONCEPTS OF HYPNOSIS *Bernard C. Gindes, M.D.*	5.00
____ NEW SELF-HYPNOSIS *Paul Adams*	5.00
____ POST-HYPNOTIC INSTRUCTIONS—Suggestions for Therapy *Arnold Furst*	3.00
____ PRACTICAL GUIDE TO SELF-HYPNOSIS *Melvin Powers*	3.00
____ PRACTICAL HYPNOTISM *Philip Magonet, M.D.*	3.00
____ SECRETS OF HYPNOTISM *S. J. Van Pelt, M.D.*	5.00
____ SELF-HYPNOSIS A Conditioned-Response Technique *Laurence Sparks*	5.00
____ SELF-HYPNOSIS Its Theory, Technique & Application *Melvin Powers*	3.00
____ THERAPY THROUGH HYPNOSIS *edited by Raphael H. Rhodes*	4.00

JUDAICA

____ MODERN ISRAEL *Lily Edelman*	2.00
____ SERVICE OF THE HEART *Evelyn Garfiel, Ph.D.*	4.00
____ STORY OF ISRAEL IN COINS *Jean & Maurice Gould*	2.00
____ STORY OF ISRAEL IN STAMPS *Maxim & Gabriel Shamir*	1.00
____ TONGUE OF THE PROPHETS *Robert St. John*	5.00

JUST FOR WOMEN

____ COSMOPOLITAN'S GUIDE TO MARVELOUS MEN Fwd. by *Helen Gurley Brown*	3.00
____ COSMOPOLITAN'S HANG-UP HANDBOOK Foreword by *Helen Gurley Brown*	4.00
____ COSMOPOLITAN'S LOVE BOOK—A Guide to Ecstasy in Bed	5.00
____ COSMOPOLITAN'S NEW ETIQUETTE GUIDE Fwd. by *Helen Gurley Brown*	4.00
____ I AM A COMPLEAT WOMAN *Doris Hagopian & Karen O'Connor Sweeney*	3.00
____ JUST FOR WOMEN—A Guide to the Female Body *Richard E. Sand, M.D.*	5.00
____ NEW APPROACHES TO SEX IN MARRIAGE *John E. Eichenlaub, M.D.*	3.00
____ SEXUALLY ADEQUATE FEMALE *Frank S. Caprio, M.D.*	3.00
____ SEXUALLY FULFILLED WOMAN *Dr. Rachel Copelan*	5.00
____ YOUR FIRST YEAR OF MARRIAGE *Dr. Tom McGinnis*	3.00

MARRIAGE, SEX & PARENTHOOD

____ ABILITY TO LOVE *Dr. Allan Fromme*	5.00
____ ENCYCLOPEDIA OF MODERN SEX & LOVE TECHNIQUES *Macandrew*	5.00

_____ GUIDE TO SUCCESSFUL MARRIAGE _Drs. Albert Ellis & Robert Harper_		5.00
_____ HOW TO RAISE AN EMOTIONALLY HEALTHY, HAPPY CHILD _A. Ellis_		4.00
_____ SEX WITHOUT GUILT _Albert Ellis, Ph.D._		5.00
_____ SEXUALLY ADEQUATE MALE _Frank S. Caprio, M.D._		3.00
_____ SEXUALLY FULFILLED MAN _Dr. Rachel Copelan_		5.00

MELVIN POWERS' MAIL ORDER LIBRARY

_____ HOW TO GET RICH IN MAIL ORDER _Melvin Powers_		15.00
_____ HOW TO WRITE A GOOD ADVERTISEMENT _Victor O. Schwab_		15.00
_____ MAIL ORDER MADE EASY _J. Frank Brumbaugh_		10.00
_____ U.S. MAIL ORDER SHOPPER'S GUIDE _Susan Spitzer_		10.00

METAPHYSICS & OCCULT

_____ BOOK OF TALISMANS, AMULETS & ZODIACAL GEMS _William Pavitt_		5.00
_____ CONCENTRATION—A Guide to Mental Mastery _Mouni Sadhu_		4.00
_____ CRITIQUES OF GOD _Edited by Peter Angeles_		7.00
_____ EXTRA-TERRESTRIAL INTELLIGENCE—The First Encounter		6.00
_____ FORTUNE TELLING WITH CARDS _P. Foli_		3.00
_____ HANDWRITING ANALYSIS MADE EASY _John Marley_		4.00
_____ HANDWRITING TELLS _Nadya Olyanova_		5.00
_____ HOW TO INTERPRET DREAMS, OMENS & FORTUNE TELLING SIGNS _Gettings_		3.00
_____ HOW TO UNDERSTAND YOUR DREAMS _Geoffrey A. Dudley_		3.00
_____ ILLUSTRATED YOGA _William Zorn_		3.00
_____ IN DAYS OF GREAT PEACE _Mouni Sadhu_		3.00
_____ LSD—THE AGE OF MIND _Bernard Roseman_		2.00
_____ MAGICIAN—His Training and Work _W. E. Butler_		3.00
_____ MEDITATION _Mouni Sadhu_		5.00
_____ MODERN NUMEROLOGY _Morris C. Goodman_		3.00
_____ NUMEROLOGY—ITS FACTS AND SECRETS _Ariel Yvon Taylor_		3.00
_____ NUMEROLOGY MADE EASY _W. Mykian_		4.00
_____ PALMISTRY MADE EASY _Fred Gettings_		3.00
_____ PALMISTRY MADE PRACTICAL _Elizabeth Daniels Squire_		4.00
_____ PALMISTRY SECRETS REVEALED _Henry Frith_		3.00
_____ PROPHECY IN OUR TIME _Martin Ebon_		2.50
_____ PSYCHOLOGY OF HANDWRITING _Nadya Olyanova_		5.00
_____ SUPERSTITION—Are You Superstitious? _Eric Maple_		2.00
_____ TAROT _Mouni Sadhu_		6.00
_____ TAROT OF THE BOHEMIANS _Papus_		5.00
_____ WAYS TO SELF-REALIZATION _Mouni Sadhu_		3.00
_____ WHAT YOUR HANDWRITING REVEALS _Albert E. Hughes_		3.00
_____ WITCHCRAFT, MAGIC & OCCULTISM—A Fascinating History _W. B. Crow_		5.00
_____ WITCHCRAFT—THE SIXTH SENSE _Justine Glass_		5.00
_____ WORLD OF PSYCHIC RESEARCH _Hereward Carrington_		2.00

SELF-HELP & INSPIRATIONAL

_____ DAILY POWER FOR JOYFUL LIVING _Dr. Donald Curtis_		5.00
_____ DYNAMIC THINKING _Melvin Powers_		2.00
_____ EXUBERANCE—Your Guide to Happiness & Fulfillment _Dr. Paul Kurtz_		3.00
_____ GREATEST POWER IN THE UNIVERSE _U. S. Andersen_		5.00
_____ GROW RICH WHILE YOU SLEEP _Ben Sweetland_		3.00
_____ GROWTH THROUGH REASON _Albert Ellis, Ph.D._		4.00
_____ GUIDE TO DEVELOPING YOUR POTENTIAL _Herbert A. Otto, Ph.D._		3.00
_____ GUIDE TO PERSONAL HAPPINESS _Albert Ellis, Ph.D. & Irving Becker, Ed. D._		5.00
_____ HELPING YOURSELF WITH APPLIED PSYCHOLOGY _R. Henderson_		2.00
_____ HELPING YOURSELF WITH PSYCHIATRY _Frank S. Caprio, M.D._		2.00
_____ HOW TO ATTRACT GOOD LUCK _A. H. Z. Carr_		4.00
_____ HOW TO DEVELOP A WINNING PERSONALITY _Martin Panzer_		5.00
_____ HOW TO DEVELOP AN EXCEPTIONAL MEMORY _Young & Gibson_		4.00
_____ HOW TO LIVE WITH A NEUROTIC _Albert Ellis, Ph. D._		5.00
_____ HOW TO OVERCOME YOUR FEARS _M. P. Leahy, M.D._		3.00
_____ HOW YOU CAN HAVE CONFIDENCE AND POWER _Les Giblin_		5.00
_____ HUMAN PROBLEMS & HOW TO SOLVE THEM _Dr. Donald Curtis_		5.00
_____ I CAN _Ben Sweetland_		5.00
_____ I WILL _Ben Sweetland_		3.00
_____ LEFT-HANDED PEOPLE _Michael Barsley_		4.00

____	MAGIC IN YOUR MIND *U. S. Andersen*	5.00
____	MAGIC OF THINKING BIG *Dr. David J. Schwartz*	3.00
____	MAGIC POWER OF YOUR MIND *Walter M. Germain*	5.00
____	MENTAL POWER THROUGH SLEEP SUGGESTION *Melvin Powers*	3.00
____	NEW GUIDE TO RATIONAL LIVING *Albert Ellis, Ph.D. & R. Harper, Ph.D.*	3.00
____	PSYCHO-CYBERNETICS *Maxwell Maltz, M.D.*	4.00
____	SCIENCE OF MIND IN DAILY LIVING *Dr. Donald Curtis*	5.00
____	SECRET OF SECRETS *U. S. Andersen*	5.00
____	SECRET POWER OF THE PYRAMIDS *U. S. Andersen*	5.00
____	STUTTERING AND WHAT YOU CAN DO ABOUT IT *W. Johnson, Ph.D.*	2.50
____	SUCCESS-CYBERNETICS *U. S. Andersen*	5.00
____	10 DAYS TO A GREAT NEW LIFE *William E. Edwards*	3.00
____	THINK AND GROW RICH *Napoleon Hill*	4.00
____	THINK YOUR WAY TO SUCCESS *Dr. Lew Losoncy*	5.00
____	THREE MAGIC WORDS *U. S. Andersen*	5.00
____	TREASURY OF COMFORT *edited by Rabbi Sidney Greenberg*	5.00
____	TREASURY OF THE ART OF LIVING *Sidney S. Greenberg*	5.00
____	YOU ARE NOT THE TARGET *Laura Huxley*	5.00
____	YOUR SUBCONSCIOUS POWER *Charles M. Simmons*	5.00
____	YOUR THOUGHTS CAN CHANGE YOUR LIFE *Dr. Donald Curtis*	5.00

SPORTS

____	BICYCLING FOR FUN AND GOOD HEALTH *Kenneth E. Luther*	2.00
____	BILLIARDS—Pocket • Carom • Three Cushion *Clive Cottingham, Jr.*	3.00
____	CAMPING-OUT 101 Ideas & Activities *Bruno Knobel*	2.00
____	COMPLETE GUIDE TO FISHING *Vlad Evanoff*	2.00
____	HOW TO IMPROVE YOUR RACQUETBALL *Lubarsky Kaufman & Scagnetti*	3.00
____	HOW TO WIN AT POCKET BILLIARDS *Edward D. Knuchell*	5.00
____	JOY OF WALKING *Jack Scagnetti*	3.00
____	LEARNING & TEACHING SOCCER SKILLS *Eric Worthington*	3.00
____	MOTORCYCLING FOR BEGINNERS *I. G. Edmonds*	3.00
____	RACQUETBALL FOR WOMEN *Toni Hudson, Jack Scagnetti & Vince Rondone*	3.00
____	RACQUETBALL MADE EASY *Steve Lubarsky, Rod Delson & Jack Scagnetti*	4.00
____	SECRET OF BOWLING STRIKES *Dawson Taylor*	3.00
____	SECRET OF PERFECT PUTTING *Horton Smith & Dawson Taylor*	3.00
____	SOCCER—The Game & How to Play It *Gary Rosenthal*	3.00
____	STARTING SOCCER *Edward F. Dolan, Jr.*	3.00

TENNIS LOVERS' LIBRARY

____	BEGINNER'S GUIDE TO WINNING TENNIS *Helen Hull Jacobs*	2.00
____	HOW TO BEAT BETTER TENNIS PLAYERS *Loring Fiske*	4.00
____	HOW TO IMPROVE YOUR TENNIS—Style, Strategy & Analysis *C. Wilson*	2.00
____	INSIDE TENNIS—Techniques of Winning *Jim Leighton*	3.00
____	PLAY TENNIS WITH ROSEWALL *Ken Rosewall*	2.00
____	PSYCH YOURSELF TO BETTER TENNIS *Dr. Walter A. Luszki*	2.00
____	SUCCESSFUL TENNIS *Neale Fraser*	3.00
____	TENNIS FOR BEGINNERS, *Dr. H. A. Murray*	2.00
____	TENNIS MADE EASY *Joel Brecheen*	3.00
____	WEEKEND TENNIS—How to Have Fun & Win at the Same Time *Bill Talbert*	3.00
____	WINNING WITH PERCENTAGE TENNIS—Smart Strategy *Jack Lowe*	2.00

WILSHIRE PET LIBRARY

____	DOG OBEDIENCE TRAINING *Gust Kessopulos*	5.00
____	DOG TRAINING MADE EASY & FUN *John W. Kellogg*	4.00
____	HOW TO BRING UP YOUR PET DOG *Kurt Unkelbach*	2.00
____	HOW TO RAISE & TRAIN YOUR PUPPY *Jeff Griffen*	3.00
____	PIGEONS: HOW TO RAISE & TRAIN THEM *William H. Allen, Jr.*	2.00

*The books listed above can be obtained from your book dealer or directly from
Melvin Powers. When ordering, please remit 50¢ per book postage & handling.
Send for our free illustrated catalog of self-improvement books.*

Melvin Powers
12015 Sherman Road, No. Hollywood, California 91605

Notes

Notes

Notes